Th
Berlin
U-Bahn

BRIAN HARDY

Capital Transport

First published 1996

ISBN 185414 184 8

Published by Capital Transport Publishing
38 Long Elmes, Harrow Weald, Middlesex

Printed by CS Graphics, Singapore

The entrance to Zoologischer Garten station in the centre of Berlin, a busy interchange between U-Bahn lines U2, U9, the S-Bahn and Regional lines. *Capital Transport*

Contents

Front cover Some 430 vehicles make up the 'D' stock fleet, built in batches between 1956 and 1971. Those on line U6 are formed of four cars, being increased to six cars in 1996 on the completion of extending the platforms formerly in East Berlin. Motor car 2093 leads at Friedrichstrasse, one of the extended stations. *Capital Transport*

Back cover Although much of the U-Bahn is in tunnel, some of it runs in the open. Much of the south-west section of U1 is in cutting, depicted here by a train of A3L.67 stock arriving at Dahlem-Dorf. *Brian Hardy*

Author's Note

This book is designed to give an appreciation and understanding of the U-Bahn (Untergrundbahn – underground railway) system in Berlin, outlining its history, development, setbacks and subsequent renaissance. The political problems, difficulties and divisions which existed for over four decades have combined to tell a remarkable story – it is hoped that this work gives readers a fair and balanced account, along with providing many useful facts and figures. For more detailed research, however, readers must read German, for there are many fine publications about both the U-Bahn and S-Bahn systems, with often one complete book being devoted to a particular subject. Readers interested in track layouts are recommended to consult the excellent track maps of Berlin by Quail.

No work of this kind is ever the result of one person's efforts and thanks are due to Jeanne Hardy for her help and support in the preparation of the book, along with Nick Agnew, Alan Blake, Ian Blee, Bob Greenaway, John Laker, Brian Patton and Steve Williams in responding to my request for photographs – the final selection has been a formidable but enjoyable task.

Your writer is most grateful to the Berlin Transport Authorities (U-Bahn), and to Bert Steinkamp (from Holland) for their assistance.

But the greatest appreciation of all must go jointly to Dr Volker Wangemann of Berlin, and Brian Patton here in Great Britain, both of whom checked the text for accuracy and researched and supplied the answers to what must have seemed a never-ending barrage of questions. Their enthusiasm and encouragement is greatly appreciated.

Ickenham, Middlesex, March 1996   BRIAN HARDY

Introduction

The Berlin U-Bahn operates two types of rolling stock on its lines. One is known as 'small profile' ("Kleinprofil"), which can be found on the original lines, and the other 'large profile' ("Grossprofil"), operating on new lines which opened from the 1920s onwards. Broadly speaking, the differences between the small and large profile trains (which are not interchangeable) are as follows:

	Small Profile	Large Profile
Car width:	2.30 metres	2.65 metres
Car Length:	12 metres	16 metres
800V dc 3rd rail current collection:	Top contact	Underside contact
Maximum speeds:	50 kph	60 kph
		(70 kph on U7 & U9)

Contrary to popular belief, there were no voltage differences on the U-Bahn in East and West Berlin, but there was a polarity difference, changed on the BVB small profile from positive to negative on 3 December 1977, which changed back to positive between 9 and 11 October 1993.

Today in Berlin there are nine U-Bahn lines – U1, U2, U4 and U15 (small profile) and U5-U9 (large profile). The 'U' prefix and line number system has been in use since 1 March 1966. Up until 1 June 1958, lines were identified by letters and (in the case of alternative branches) by (Roman) numbers. In the intervening eight years there was no system for line identification for passenger information, other than the ultimate destinations of each line, which was deemed sufficient for the travelling public. There was, however, one exception – line E in East Berlin continued to 'exist' in that form. The authorities, however, continued to use the old system for internal purposes.

Berlin U-Bahn History

In the Beginning – Trams Before Trains

Like the Liverpool Overhead Railway in Great Britain, the Hochbahn Company in Berlin sought to extend its sphere of influence by the construction of a tram line. This initially ran from Warschauer Brücke to Zentralviehof and was opened for traffic even before the U-Bahn itself, on 1 October 1901. It was sold to the Strassenbahnen der Stadt Berlin (Tramways of the City of Berlin) on 1 January 1910. The Hochbahn then transferred the cars to a new line from Warschauer Brücke to Frankfurter Allee Ringbahn station, which went into service on the same date. On 1 July 1913 this was extended to Wagnerplatz in Lichtenberg. When the flat fare of 20 Pf was introduced on 15 March 1927, the line was numbered 90. Until then it had been known as Flachbahn der Hochbahn (Surface Line of the Elevated Railway). On 1 April 1928 it was incorporated into the main Berlin system and today it is part of route 23.

The original trams were built by Siemens and were eight in number. Unlike the majority of Berlin trams, they were fitted with bow collectors, rather than trolley poles. They were transferred to the new line in 1910. In 1926 five modern motor cars and nine trailers, to the design of the main tram system's class T24, were obtained. Other motor and trailer cars were obtained at an earlier date from Breslau and, probably, Düsseldorf.

Original entrance to Wittenbergplatz, then spelt as two words.

The Small Profile Lines

The Berlin U-Bahn owes much of its creation and development to Werner von Siemens. After the success of his first electric railway at the Berlin exhibition of 1879, he prepared plans to serve the city by a network of electric lines running on viaducts. The first of these would have run the length of Friedrichstrasse on separate viaducts mounted above the pavement on each side of the street, at first-floor level, and the lines would have been of metre gauge. Not surprisingly, there was considerable public outcry at the prospect and Wilhelm I refused the Royal Assent, without which the scheme could not proceed. Instead, von Siemens turned his attention to tramways and in 1881 opened the world's first electric tramway at Lichterfelde.

However, the idea of a rapid transit system remained alive and in 1891 the firm of Siemens und Halske published a plan for an east-west line from Warschauer Strasse in the east to Zoologischer Garten in the west, with a branch northwards to Potsdamer Platz. With interchange to the Stadtbahn at both ends, such a line would neatly complement the Stadtbahn, which had avoided much of the built-up area. The line was to be of standard gauge and would run on viaduct throughout its length. In 1893, Wilhelm II, who had rather more interest in matters technical than his grandfather had shown, finally gave his assent for the section from Warschauer Brücke to Nollendorfplatz and the branch to Potsdamer Platz. There had been some concern about the impact of an overhead line in certain areas, particularly Auguste-Viktoria-Platz (Breitscheidplatz) and only after it was agreed to build that part underground was permission given in 1897 for the western section. Very soon, an underground extension northwards from Potsdamer Platz through the very centre of the city to Spittelmarkt was added to the plans, as was one from Zoologischer Garten to Knie *(now Ernst-Reuter-Platz)*.

Stralauer Tor, located between Schlesisches Tor and Warschauer Brücke, was permanently closed in 1945 after destruction by bombing.

As Berlin was still a collection of separate municipalities, negotiations had then to be undertaken with those affected – Berlin, Schöneberg and Charlottenburg and also with the main line railways (KPEV). The legal basis for the line was to be the Light Railway Act of 1892.

Finally, early in 1896, the negotiations were concluded and Siemens & Halske, together with the Deutsche Bank, formed on 13 April 1897 the Gesellschaft für elektrische Hoch-und Untergrundbahnen in Berlin – normally referred to as the Hoch-bahn-Gesellschaft. This translated to the Berlin Elevated and Underground Electric Railway Company. This firm received a concession for 90 years, but Siemens & Halske were to operate the line for the first year for their own account, against a payment of 4% of the capital, which was 12.5-million Mark. Trains were to run at not more than 50 km/hr. For the first seven years, the Company was to have complete freedom to fix fares and for the first three, the timetable. A 10-minute service would operate to each destination from each, giving each section a combined 5-minute interval service.

Construction began even before the Company was formed, on 10 September 1896. Progress was generally rapid, but there were considerable difficulties with the triangular junction (Gleisdreieck) and it was not until September 1901 that trial running could begin. A depot and workshop was built on the south-east side of the line between Stralauer Tor and Warschauer Brücke, nearer to the latter, and the power station and another depot were located at Trebbiner Strasse, very close to the site of the present Museum für Verkher und Technik.

The official opening took place on 15 February 1902 but the initial sections of railway were opened to the public in five stages, as follows:

18 February 1902	Stralauer Tor *(latterly known as Osthafen but closed permanently in 1945)*– Potsdamer Platz
11 March 1902	Potsdamer Platz–Zoologischer Garten
25 March 1902	Bülowstrasse–Möckernbrücke (direct line which linked Zoologischer Garten with Stralauer Tor)
17 August 1902	Stralauer Tor–Warschauer Brücke *(present name Warschauer Strasse)*
14 December 1902	Zoologischer Garten–Knie *(present name Ernst-Reuter-Platz)*

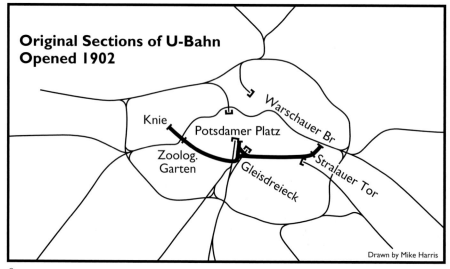

Original Sections of U-Bahn Opened 1902

Drawn by Mike Harris

But extensions and new lines were already planned and some were already under construction. These now comprise the present lines U1, U2, U4 and U15 and the erstwhile line U5, which is not to be confused with the present line U5. These extensions took place over a seven-year period and saw the initial system grow from 11.2 km to 35 km. On the eastern side of the city, there were two destinations – Warschauer Brücke and Nordring *(now Schönhauser Allee),* the latter extended in stages from Potsdamer Platz. Westwards, there became a choice of five routes and destinations.

Even before the line was opened, in 1900, the municipality of Charlottenburg – which seems to have been the most enthusiastic of the three involved – had suggested a further extension westwards, from Knie to Wilhelmplatz *(now Richard-Wagner-Platz).* This extension was opened on 14 May 1906 – all underground. This served one intermediate station of Bismarckstrasse which, after four renamings, became the present Deutsche Oper station. The station was built with two island platforms and four tracks.

The Deutsche Bank was closely connected with an estate development company, the Neu-Westend-Gesellschaft (New West End Company), which had been formed to develop the area around Bismarckstrasse and Westend, and this led to plans for a further extension westwards. Construction began in 1906 and the line from Bismarckstrasse *(Deutsche Oper)* to Reichskanzlerplatz *(Theodor-Heuss-Platz)* was opened by Wilhelm II on 29 March 1908. This was the first time that he had actually travelled on the U-Bahn, despite his interest in transport, and the saloon in which he rode was afterwards known as the "Kaiserwagen". The section between Bismarckstrasse and Wilhelmplatz then became a separate shuttle service. The extension was entirely underground, but just east of Kaiserdamm, the line – in tunnel – passes over the Ringbahn and it is just visible through gaps in the girder work.

The original station at Potsdamer Platz, opened on 18 February 1902, was closed and resited 180 metres to the north on 28 September 1907, because of the construction of the new department store Wertheim and to give better interchange to the Fürstenhof Hotel. The new station opened as Leipziger Platz but reverted to Potsdamer Platz in 1923. There were considerable difficulties with construction of the extension northwards to Spittelmarkt, where the station was situated on the edge of the River Spree, but these were eventually overcome and the line was opened for traffic on 1 October 1908.

14.

Nollendorfplatz, 1902

Meanwhile, the municipality of Schöneberg had begun to consider having its own system and, after toying with the idea of a Schwebebahn, Wuppertal-style, decided instead on an underground line. This was to run from Nollendorfplatz to Hauptstrasse *(now Innsbrucker Platz)*, a distance of just 3 km. Construction began in 1909 and the line was opened on 1 December 1910. Schöneberg could then pride itself on being the fifth European city to have an electric underground railway. As befitted a well-to-do area, the stations were well finished, that at Viktoria-Luise-Platz having especially fine entrances. Stadtpark station *(now Rathaus Schöneberg)* was constructed at ground level but within a concrete shell with windows at the sides open to daylight from the adjacent park. This independent line boasted its own depot at Eisackstrasse, south of Hauptstrasse, and was initially wholly self-contained with no connections to the other lines. However, its 12 motor coaches were identical to those of the Hochbahn and this made their transfer, on 10 July 1926, an easy matter.

The increase in traffic brought about by the extensions, taxed the capacity of the triangular junction at Gleisdreieck and in 1907 it was decided to rebuild this into an interchange station, with lines on separate levels, and also to build a relief line between that point and Nollendorfplatz via Kurfürstenstrasse. Further impetus to these plans was given by a sidelong collision at Gleisdreieck on 26 September 1908, when one train overran a red signal and collided with another. One coach ended up in the yard below of the power station and there were several fatalities. The new station opened on 3 November 1912, from which date the south curve closed – the north curve had previously closed on 25 July 1912. The original depot here was closed. Trains running direct between Bülowstrasse and Leipziger Platz served the new first-level elevated station, while trains from Warschauer Brücke terminated in the even higher-level platforms, set at right-angles to the one below. It was to be another 14 years before the extension to Wittenbergplatz via Kurfürstenstrasse was realised. Single line connections were retained in the directions Möckernbrücke to Leipziger Platz and Bülowstrasse to Möckernbrücke.

The growth in the rolling stock fleet also taxed the capacity of the workshops at Warschauer Brücke and it was decided to build a new depot and workshop on 14 hectares of land at Grunewald, to the west of the existing terminus of Reichskanzlerplatz. The workshops were opened in January 1913 and trains ran empty to and from the terminus. Adjacent to the new depot, a new station, known as Stadion *(now Olympia Stadion [Ost])*, was built to serve the stadium and from 8 June 1913, trains were extended to serve this on occasions of sporting fixtures and special events. The new line was in tunnel until just before the station and the depot.

In 1910 work began on a northward extension from Spittelmarkt to Nordring *(now Schönhauser Allee)*, via Alexanderplatz. This involved some very difficult tunnelling, in the course of which some of the original fortifications and a powder magazine of the early settlement of Berlin/Cölln were discovered. There was also an episode of flooding, when water not only overflowed the tunnelling works but also the section between Leipziger Platz and Spittelmarkt. The line was extended to Alexanderplatz on 1 July 1913 and on to Nordring on 27 July. Between Senefelderplatz and Danziger Strasse *(now Eberswalder Strasse)* the line climbed onto an elevated structure, on which it ran to the terminus. There were also plans to build a branch from Klosterstrasse to Frankfurter Allee and to provide for this, the former station was laid out on very spacious lines, with room for a third track in the middle. The proposed line would have run via Königstrasse, crossing the line to Pankow at Alexanderplatz.

A short (1.195 km) branch was opened from Wittenbergplatz to Uhlandstrasse on 12 October 1913. This was built at the suggestion of the municipality of Charlottenburg, which provided a grant of 2-million Mark towards its construction. This line was intended to be the first stage of an extension to Grunewald via Halensee.

Apart from the extension to Grunewald, serving the new workshops, all lines built up to this time had traversed areas which were already densely populated. However, to the south-west lay an area ripe for housing development and the municipality of Wilmersdorf was anxious to have this area connected to the city by a branch of the U-Bahn. Work began at Wittenbergplatz in October 1909, with the rebuilding of that station into a junction, with two new platforms – the present attractive station building dates from this time, although recently restored. Construction through marshy ground in Wilmersdorf was not easy and part of the line in this area had to be built within a concrete shell. The Hochbahn built the section from Wittenbergplatz to Nürnberger Platz, Wilmersdorf built the section from there to Breitenbachplatz and the remainder of the line was financed by the Prussian Ministry of Finance. Operation, however, was by the Hochbahn throughout. The stations, for the first time in the U-Bahn's development, were designed as architectural features and that at Dahlem-Dorf, at the suggestion of Wilhelm II (probably in one of his Anglophile moments) was built as a thatched cottage. There were eight intermediate stations and the line was in the open air from Podbielskiallee to Thielplatz, where a small temporary workshop was built at the latter. This line was also opened for traffic on 12 October 1913 (although the section between Fehrbelliner Platz and Thielplatz operated as a separate shuttle until Krumme Lanke was reached in 1929).

There was then a hiatus in U-Bahn development due, in part, to the First World War, and it was not until 1919 that construction work was resumed – on both extensions and new lines. Insofar as new lines were concerned, these were to be built henceforth to the larger profile and will be covered below under the relevant section.

To further broaden its sphere of influence and in particular to cater for north-south traffic, the Hochbahn formed in 1914 a subsidiary undertaking, the Hochbahn-Omnibus-Gesellschaft mbH (Elevated Railway Omnibus Co. Ltd). This acquired 60 open-top double-deck buses, of much the same design as were then being built for the ABOAG. To distinguish them from the buses of the latter, the Hochbahn buses were painted blue and yellow. Services began in May 1914 on the following routes:

AI	Stettiner Bahnhof–Hermannplatz
AII	Stettiner Bahnhof–Neu-Tempelhof
B	Bahnhof Prenzlauer Allee–Bahnhof Hermannstrasse

Each service called at several U-Bahn stations en route and transfer tickets were available. Services had to end on 12 August 1914 and when they were finally restarted in 1921 (service A) and 1924 (B), they were run by the ABOAG.

Returning now to the U-Bahn, the first post-war event on the small profile network was in fact the construction of a new underground station between Reichskanzlerplatz and Stadion. Named Neu-Westend, it opened to the public on 20 May 1922. At the same time, short workings to Reichskanzlerplatz were discontinued and a regular through service to Stadion was provided.

The much-needed and second route was at last provided from Gleisdreieck to Wittenbergplatz via Kurfürstenstrasse from 24 October 1926. Crossing the platform below at right angles at Gleisdreieck, the new extension passed over a large girder bridge before going into tunnel. The first part of this tunnel in fact crosses Dennewitzstrasse and at that point it is an above-ground fully-encased concrete tunnel above the street! The new tunnel station at Nollendorfplatz also provided same level interchange with the branch line of the Schöneberger Untergrundbahn and that line's original platforms at Nollendorfplatz, hitherto unconnected to the rest of the network, were closed at the same time.

On the original (elevated) section of line, Kottbusser Tor station was resited 100 metres to the west on 4 August 1929, to provide more convenient interchange with the recently opened (on 12 February 1928) large profile line, which later became U8.

The completion of the small profile network was achieved during 1929 and 1930. An extension from Stadion to Ruhleben was opened on 22 December 1929, when the former station was also rebuilt with two island platforms serving three tracks, to provide for easier handling of crowds attending sporting events and for trains entering and leaving service there. On the same date, a 3.1 km extension of the Wilmersdorfer U-Bahn was opened from Thielplatz to Krumme Lanke, from which time through services were operated instead of a shuttle to and from Fehrbelliner Platz. In connection with this extension, the Prussian Treasury consigned to the city of Berlin the part of the line which it had owned and also gave a grant of 850,000 Mark towards the construction costs. Land for the new line was given by the developers Sommerfeld, who were planning new housing in the area and, as they also paid for the fitting out of the extension, the city of Berlin got a new U-Bahn line for minimal outlay! A new depot and workshops, with staff housing, were built at Krumme Lanke which replaced the temporary facilities at Thielplatz. The extension attracted much excursion and leisure traffic and sometimes handled 40,000 people on a fine day.

The last section of all to be opened in this era was one station north, 1.2 km long on 29 June 1930, from Nordring to Pankow (Vinetastrasse). This extension from Nordring continued for a short distance on viaduct before going underground to the new terminus.

At this time, train service route identification on the narrow profile lines was changed from (Roman) numbering to include letters and then (Roman) numbers. They were as follows:

Line	Between
AI	Pankow (Vinetastrasse)–Ruhleben via Bülowstrasse
AII	Pankow (Vinetastrasse)–Krumme Lanke via Bülowstrasse
AIII	Städtische Oper *(originally Bismarckstrasse and now Deutsche Oper)*–Wilhelm Platz *(now Richard-Wagner-Platz)*
BI	Warschauer Brücke–Hauptstrasse *(now Innsbrucker Platz)*
BII	Warschauer Brücke–Uhlandstrasse

From then on until the present day, the extent of these lines changed little, apart from those that were affected by the construction of the Wall in August 1961 (q.v. below), although patterns of operation changed to meet traffic demands.

Readers will be aware of the mass destruction that occurred in Berlin during the Second World War, and how it affected the S-Bahn network. The U-Bahn, too, fared no better, and the complete system came to a halt by mid-April 1945. Prior to that, because of air raid damage, the station at Osthafen *(originally Stralauer Tor)*, located between Schlesisches Tor and Warschauer Brücke – a short distance from the latter – closed on 10 March 1945, never to be reopened.

After the capitulation on 8 May 1945, the U-Bahn made a remarkable recovery. The first section to reopen did so on 14 May 1945 on the large profile system and the complete details will be found in the relevant sections. Suffice to say that service restoration throughout the network took until 1947 to complete with some lines having to operate a multiplicity of shuttle services before through running could be achieved. The last of the closed stations reopened in 1951, the same year as the last section of single track was restored to double track.

The U-Bahn System on 18 April 1930

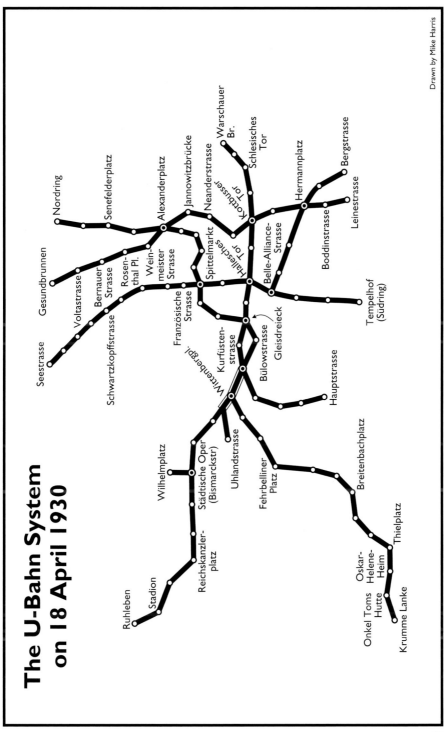

Drawn by Mike Harris

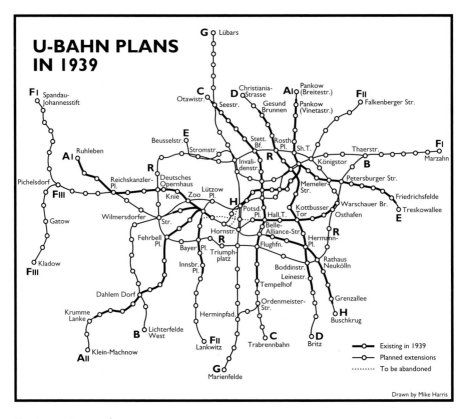

U-BAHN PLANS IN 1939

Drawn by Mike Harris

Post-war Reopenings

In the list that follows, the present U-Bahn line numbers have been used, to enable a better understanding of the routes involved. An asterisk indicates that the service operated was a shuttle. Note, however, that line U5 shown § was closed in 1970.

Line	Date	Sections Reopened/Operated
U2	17.05.45	*Knie (Ernst-Reuter-Platz)–Kaiserdamm
U2	17.05.45	Kaiserdamm–Ruhleben
U5§	18.05.45	Richard-Wagner-Platz–Deutsches Opernhaus (Deutsche Oper)–single track
U2	24.05.45	*Knie–Deutsches Opernhaus
U2	24.05.45	Deutsches Opernhaus–Ruhleben
U2	31.05.45	*Schönhauser Allee–Alexanderplatz
U2	31.05.45	Zoologischer Garten–Knie (* a shuttle between Zoologischer Garten and Deutsches Opernhaus)
U1	07.06.45	*Hohenzollernplatz–Rüdesheimer Platz
U1	07.06.45	*Breitenbachplatz–Thielplatz
U1	08.06.45	*Thielplatz–Krumme Lanke
U1	11.06.45	*Schlesisches Tor–Prinzenstrasse
U1	21.06.45	Rüdesheimer Platz–Breitenbachplatz (* actually a shuttle between Hohenzollernplatz and Breitenbachplatz)
U1	24.06.45	*Kurfürstenstrasse–Wittenbergplatz

Line	Date	Sections Reopened/Operated
U4	24.06.45	*Nollendorfplatz–Bayerischer Platz
U1	01.07.45	Breitenbachplatz–Krumme Lanke (replacing two shuttles Breitenbachplatz–Thielplatz and Thielplatz–Krumme Lanke)
U1	15.07.45	Wittenbergplatz–Nürnberger Platz (* a shuttle Kurfürstenstrasse–Nürnberger Platz)
U2	15.07.45	Wittenbergplatz–Zoologischer Garten (* actually a shuttle Wittenbergplatz–Deutsches Opernhaus)
U15	23.07.45	Wittenbergplatz–Uhlandstrasse (* actually a shuttle Kurfürstenstrasse–Uhlandstrasse)
U2	26.07.45	Through service Wittenbergplatz–Ruhleben, replacing split services Wittenbergplatz–Deutsches-Opernhaus shuttle and Deutsches-Opernhaus Ruhleben
U2	30.07.45	*Stadtmitte–Potsdamer Platz (Kaiserhof remains closed)
U2	31.07.45	*Märkisches Museum–Stadtmitte (Hausvogteiplatz station remains closed)
U2	01.08.45	Pankow (Vinetastrasse)–Schönhauser Allee (with through service Pankow (Vinetastrasse)–Alexanderplatz)
U2	01.08.45	*Alexanderplatz–Klosterstrasse
U1	17.08.45	*Hohenzollernplatz–Fehrbelliner Platz and Fehrbelliner Platz–Krumme Lanke replaces Breitenbachplatz–Krumme Lanke and shuttles Hohenzollernplatz–Rüdesheimer Platz and Rüdesheimer Platz–Breitenbachplatz
U1	21.09.45	Nürnberger Platz–Hohenzollernplatz (* actually a shuttle Nürnberger Platz–Fehrbelliner Platz)
U1	06.10.45	Through service Wittenbergplatz–Krumme Lanke, replaces Fehbelliner Platz–Krumme Lanke and shuttles Hohenzollernplatz–Rüdesheimer Platz and Rüdesheimer Platz–Breitenbachplatz. Note that shuttle Kurfürstenstrasse–Uhlandstrasse still operates
U1	14.10.45	Prinzenstrasse–Hallesches Tor and Warschauer Brücke–Schlesisches Tor, double tracked with exception of Warschauer Brücke–Schesisches Tor and Hallesches Tor stations
U15	21.10.45	Wittenbergplatz–Uhlandstrasse – single line shuttle
U1	21.10.45	Gleisdreieck–Kurfürstenstrasse (actually through service Gleisdreieck–Ruhleben via Kurfürstenstrasse)
U2	01.11.45	*Klosterstrasse–Märkisches Museum plus shuttles Klosterstrasse–Spittelmarkt and Spittelmarkt–Stadtmitte, replacing shuttle Märkisches Museum–Spittelmarkt
U2	15.11.45	Through service Pankow (Vinetastrasse)–Potsdamer Platz, replacing Pankow (Vinetastrasse)–Alexanderplatz and four shuttles Alexanderplatz–Klosterstrasse, Klosterstrasse–Spittelmarkt, Spittelmarkt–Stadtmitte and Stadtmitte–Potsdamer Platz
U2	18.11.45	*Potsdamer Platz–Gleisdreieck
U2	24.11.45	Through service Pankow (Vinetastrasse)–Gleisdreieck, replacing Pankow (Vinetastrasse)–Potsdamer Platz and shuttle Potsdamer Platz–Gleisdreieck
U4	06.12.45	*Bayerischer Platz–Innsbrucker Platz (Stadtpark station remains closed)
U4	15.09.46	Through service Nollendorfplatz–Innsbrucker Platz
U2	15.09.46	Gleisdreieck–Wittenbergplatz via Bülowstrasse reopened with Nollendorfplatz remaining closed, enabling a through service Pankow (Vinetastrasse)–Ruhleben
U15	15.09.46	Through service reinstated Gleisdreieck–Uhlandstrasse via Kurfürstenstrasse
U1	27.04.47	Hallesches Tor–Gleisdreieck with through service Warschauer Brücke–Uhlandstrasse, Möckernbrücke remains closed
U2	24.05.47	Nollendorfplatz (high level) station reopened
U1	16.06.47	Möckernbrücke station reopened
U5§	01.11.47	Richard-Wagner-Platz–Deutsches Opernhaus double tracked
U1	15.10.49	Hallesches Tor station double tracked
U2	07.01.50	Hausvogteiplatz station reopened
U2	18.08.50	Thälmannplatz (previously Kaiserhof) station reopened
U4	15.05.51	Rathaus Schöneberg (Stadtpark) station reopened
U1	12.12.51	Schlesisches Tor–Warschauer Brücke double tracked

When closed in 1972, Bülowstrasse station subsequently became a Turkish Bazaar. *Nick Agnew*

In post-war times, construction of line G (what is now line U9) began in 1955 and the interchanges proposed affected both lines AII and BII. A new station was to be built on line G at Kurfürstendamm, which crossed under line BII at that location, then without a station. To enable both lines to benefit from a station there, the section Wittenbergplatz–Uhlandstrasse closed on 18 November 1957.

Interchange between line G and AII was to be provided at Spichernstrasse. This involved the construction of another two new stations and the closure of one, but without any major line disruption. The new Spichernstrasse station, then only serving line AII, replaced Nürnberger Platz on 2 June 1959 while slightly to the north-west, a new station, Augsburger Strasse, opened on 8 May 1961. This new station (between Spichernstrasse and Wittenbergplatz) was necessary because of what would have been a long distance (1.106 km) between the two. The sidings east of Spichernstrasse are on the site of the former Nürnberger Platz station. Line BII between Wittenbergplatz and Uhlandstrasse, complete with a new intermediate station at Kurfürstendamm, reopened on 2 September 1961, although the new line G serving there had opened five days earlier on 28 August.

By this time, the operation of the small profile lines had contracted by the building of the Wall, which divided East and West Berlin for over 28 years from 13 August 1961. Because of this, lines BI and BII were closed and abandoned beyond Schlesisches Tor to Warschauer Brücke, including the depot at the latter. Lines AI and AII were split in two, terminating in West Berlin at Gleisdreieck and in East Berlin at Thälmannplatz *(originally Kaiserhof, later Otto-Grotewohl-Strasse and now Mohrenstrasse)*. Potsdamer Platz station was closed. Interestingly, East Berlin trains could be stabled west of Thälmannplatz as far as Potsdamer Platz station (which was just in West Berlin) but the station entrances there stayed firmly closed! In all, therefore, just two small profile stations were closed at that stage – Warschauer Brücke and Potsdamer Platz. The line in East Berlin (along with the large profile line E, wholly in East Berlin), were operated by BVG East and those in West Berlin by BVG West.

From 1 March 1966, West Berlin U-Bahn services were reorganised and lines were given numbers, each prefixed by the letter 'U'. The small profile lines then became:

Line	Between
U1	Schlesisches Tor–Ruhleben via Kurfürstenstrasse
U2	Gleisdreieck–Krumme Lanke via Bülowstrasse
U3	Wittenbergplatz–Uhlandstrasse
U4	Nollendorfplatz–Innsbrucker Platz *(previously Hauptstrasse)*
U5	Deutsche Oper *(originally Bismarckstrasse)*–Richard-Wagner-Platz *(previously Wilhelmplatz)*

In East Berlin, the section between Thälmannplatz and Pankow (Vinetastrasse) reverted to the line route identification 'A'.

To facilitate construction work for extensions of what became line U7, the service between Deutsche Oper and Richard-Wagner-Platz, which had been a shuttle since 13 August 1961, closed on 2 May 1970. A new station, Bismarckstrasse, 0.38 km west of Deutsche Oper, was eventually opened on line U1 on 28 April 1978 at the same time as line U7, the latter restoring a service to Richard-Wagner-Platz, albeit on a slightly different route.

The section of line U2 between Gleisdreieck and Wittenbergplatz was abandoned from 1 January 1972, with services to and from Krumme Lanke cut back to the latter. This was because there were two routes between Gleisdreieck and Wittenbergplatz (one via Kurfürstenstrasse, the other via Bülowstrasse) and the traffic offering on the latter could not justify the retention of both. Two elevated viaduct stations, Bülowstrasse and Nollendorfplatz, also closed at the same time, while the lower (but still elevated) platforms at Gleisdreieck, devoid of a train service, remained as access between the high level station and the street.

Not all the abandoned sections of line or stations were left to lay derelict, however. At Nollendorfplatz, a flea market was established in the high level station in 1973 and 16 small profile U-Bahn carriages were equipped to sell various types of goods. At Bülowstrasse there was a Turkish bazaar. One track of the elevated section between Nollendorfplatz and Bülowstrasse was equipped with overhead line equipment and a vintage West Berlin tram commenced operation on 16 March 1978 – the tram linked the two stations at a rather leisurely pace.

A further section of the abandoned line U2 was put to use in the form of the M-Bahn (Magnetbahn). This was from Gleisdreieck and headed north for about 0.5 km where it diverged westwards. The sad and sorry story of this bold experiment will be told later, its fate being sealed after reunification, when the restoration of the through service on line U2 was authorised.

At the time, however, there was nothing to suggest that the division between East and West Berlin would not continue, but to the surprise of everyone world-wide on 9 November 1989, the division came to a very sudden and very welcome end with the opening of the frontier crossings. On the two large profile lines concerned (U6 and U8 – q.v. below) it was necessary only to reopen closed stations, but with lines U1 and U2 much costly work needed to be done to get the closed sections operational again. Priority was given to the Wittenbergplatz-Mohrenstrasse *(previously Otto-Grotewohl-Strasse)* section of U2. This involved removing the flea market and 16 U-Bahn carriages from Nollendorfplatz, the Turkish Bazaar at Bülowstrasse, the vintage tramway and overhead wire supports between the two, and the M-Bahn running north from Gleisdreieck. The vintage tram ceased operation on 15 April 1991, following which the U-Bahn carriages were removed from Nollendorfplatz in June. The M-Bahn ceased operation on 31 July 1991 and dismantling it took place between September 1991 and January 1992. Only then was work able to start in restoring the missing link, including the construction of certain new sections of overhead structure. The section of line between Mohrenstrasse and Alexanderplatz was also closed from 13 April to 3 October 1992, for modernisation and reconditioning. The actual 'gap' between Potsdamer Platz and Gleisdreieck was bridged on 2 March 1993 and trial running of trains commenced on 17 July 1993.

The section between Wittenbergplatz and Mohrenstrasse reopened to passenger traffic on line U2, some four years after the division of the city had ended – from 13 November 1993. From that date, services on lines U1, U2 and U3 were reorganised and recast. Line U1 from Schlesisches Tor was diverted at Wittenbergplatz to serve the south-west terminus of Krumme Lanke, while U3 between Uhlandstrasse and Wittenbergplatz became U15 and was extended eastwards to Schlesisches Tor in the peaks and on Saturdays 08.00 to 09.00 and to Kottbusser Tor midday off-peak Monday to Friday and 09.00 to 14.00 on Saturday. At other times, the line U15 continued to operate as a shuttle. Line U2 from Vinetastrasse, via the reopened section between Mohrenstrasse and Wittenbergplatz, served the north-west route to Ruhleben.

The last section of U-Bahn to reopen because of the Wall was the section between Schlesisches Tor and Warschauer Brücke, on which work was completed in October 1995. The overhead structure, having lain derelict for some 34 years, has been rebuilt and restored to near original condition, along with the depot and former terminus, where improved interchange with the S-Bahn at Warschauer Strasse has been provided. Reopening took place on 14 October 1995 from which date the U-Bahn station became known as Warschauer Strasse, to match that of the nearby S-Bahn station. Serving lines U1 and U15 this makes the small profile network almost similar to what it was when completed in 1930, save for the 1.4 km section between Deutsche Oper and Richard-Wagner-Platz, now used as one of the two connections between the small and large profile networks.

There is but one extension of the narrow profile network under construction, north from Vinetastrasse *(previously Pankow [Vinetastrasse])* to Pankow Kirche. At present, the tunnel is complete up to the point where it crosses the S-Bahn at Pankow, but the remaining section to Pankow Kirche is outstanding to be completed, making an opening date of 1997 looking unlikely. Further, a new depot planned on this extension at Granitzstrasse is now unlikely to be built.

More long-term projects may see U1 extended from Warschauer Brücke to Friedrich-shain and from Krumme Lanke to Mexikoplatz, U2 extended from Ruhleben to Rathaus Spandau (where provision has already been made at the latter) and from Pankow to Nordend. Line U15 (previously U3) may become a cross-city line from Theodor-Heuss-Platz to Alexanderplatz and then possibly into the eastern suburbs.

After some 34 years of closure and neglect, the 803-metre section between Schlesisches Tor and Warschauer Brücke reopened on 14 October 1995. Happily, the overhead structure has been restored to its former glory, as seen here between the two stations in September 1995. *Capital Transport*

By July 1995, the reconstruction of Warschauer Brücke station (which was renamed Warschauer Strasse on reopening), was taking shape, as seen here. The depot is also being revived and the building can be seen in the far background. *Brian Hardy*

When the section of line U1 to Warschauer Brücke closed in 1961, the immediate area became a 'no-man's land' and what remained stayed untouched. After the frontiers were re-opened, it became possible again to walk what had become a derelict area. The first photograph, on 6 September 1992, shows the old signal box at Warschauer Brücke and the overall roof of the station in the background. On re-opening day, 14 October 1995, the signal box is shown straddling the track at Warschauer Strasse. *Alan Blake, Dr Volker Wangemann*

A view from the high-level platform on line U1 at Gleisdreieck, looking north on 29 June 1994. Two mixed livery trains of G stock pass each other on the recently reopened section of line U2, while to the left, the remains of the alignment of S-Bahn tracks into Potsdamer Ringbahnhof can be seen. *Brian Hardy*

After passing over the girder bridge, the line crosses Dennewitzstrasse which is encased in a 'tunnel' and then proceeds in the basement of flats (left). This view of the enclosed bridge was taken on 4 September 1992. *Alan Blake*

A train of G stock descends the ramp between Schönhauser Allee and Pankow (Vinetastrasse) on 22 June 1993. To the right can be seen the poles supporting overhead wires for trams. This was the last section of the narrow profile network to open in 1930. *Steve Williams*

The Gleisdreieck–Wittenbergplatz section of U2 closed on 1 January 1972 and remained so for another 21 years. This view looks west from Nollendorfplatz. *Nick Agnew*

This section of line U2 reopened in November 1993. Looking west in September 1995, a train of the more modern A3L stock emerges from the tunnel between Wittenbergplatz and Nollendorfplatz. *Capital Transport*

Above Between the flea market at Nollendorfplatz and the Turkish Bazaar at Bülowstrasse, a vintage West Berlin 4-wheeled tram operated on the eastbound disused track after the installation of supporting poles and overhead wires. This view was taken on 25 May 1986. *John Laker*

Below left The first M-Bahn vehicle to operate on test was built by MBB and was numbered 706, running from June 1984 until October 1986, and is seen on 25 May 1986 at Gleisdreieck. *John Laker*

Below right Vehicle 04, built by Waggon-Union, at Gleisdreieck after the fitting of platform edge doors. This, along with cars 06 and 07, were removed in September 1991. *Nick Agnew*

The Large Profile Lines

Even while the original network was being developed, it was realised that the small profile and the car width of 2.30 metres would be a hindrance to future growth of traffic. The lines of the Hochbahn also had the disadvantage that they served basically the east-west axis of the city, also served by the Stadtbahn, while north-south traffic flows were handled by the tramways. The municipality of Berlin therefore resolved to build two north-south lines in its own right and to construct these to a wider loading gauge, to allow the operation of cars 2.65 metres wide.

These lines would be:

A Nordsüdbahn running from Seestrasse to Belle-Alliance-Strasse (*Mehringdamm*) via Friedrichstrasse, with possible extensions from the latter terminus to Tempelhof and Neukölln.

A line from Gesundbrunnen to Neukölln via Alexanderplatz.

There were also plans for a third new line, from Görlitzer Bahnhof to Moabit, which would serve areas to the north of the Stadtbahn, but due to the outbreak of the First World War, this project was not pursued.

A further difference was that trains on the new lines would take current either from overhead lines or from an under-running third rail. In the event, the choice fell on the latter.

Permission for the first line was obtained from the authorities in 1912 and work began almost immediately. It continued until 1917, despite increasingly difficult conditions. As male labour became shorter, women were employed. It was also necessary to lay rails in the streets, to allow military transport to continue during excavations – these lines were also used to bring in materials and remove spoil. Finally, the works were stopped in 1917, although two sections had been almost completed. In 1921, it was proposed to abandon the line permanently but it was found that the cost of doing so would be almost as great as completion of the half-finished sections. In the following year, therefore, the new municipality of Greater Berlin established the Nordsüdbahn AG to complete and open for traffic the almost-completed sections.

Despite the raging inflation, work was resumed and the first section from Stettiner Bahnhof *(now Zinnowitzer Strasse)* to Hallesches Tor, a distance of 4 km, was opened for traffic on 30 January 1923. As stated elsewhere, it had to be worked by modified trains from the small profile network. Quite apart from the financial problems, construction was complicated by the necessity to tunnel under both the Spree and the Landwehrkanal and to underpin and reconstruct the foundations of Friedrichstrasse station without interruption to the S-Bahn or main line trains. The line was extended northwards to its terminus at Seestrasse on 8 March 1923, with access to a new depot and workshops. These were constructed on land given by the municipality and were not fully operational until 1925. Extensions southwards then followed and in 1924 reached Gneisenaustrasse on 19 April and Hasenheide *(now Südstern)* on 14 December. Other opening dates in this era were:

Date	Between
14 February 1926	Belle-Alliance-Strasse (now Mehringdamm)–Kreuzberg (now Platz der Luftbrücke)
11 April 1926	Hasenheide (now Südstern)–Bergstrasse (now Karl-Marx-Strasse)
10 September 1927	Kreuzberg–Flughafen (now Paradestrasse)
22 December 1929	Flughafen–Tempelhof (Südring)
21 December 1930	Tempelhof (Südring)–Grenzallee

The last-mentioned opening date (which also applied to new line E, q.v. below), was the last extension to the U-Bahn system for some 26 years. This line had two routes, being CI (Seestrasse – Grenzallee) and CII (Seestrasse – Tempelhof [Südring]).

Planning of the second north-south line dated back to 1905, when the Continentale Gesellschaft für elektrische Unternehmungen (Continental Electrical Undertaking Company), which was based in Nürnberg, proposed a suspended Schwebebahn, Wuppertal style, for which a test track was constructed in Brunnenstrasse in 1906. It existed until 1913. However, the Berlin authorities had little enthusiasm for the idea and plans passed to the AEG company, who proposed a conventional underground line. To construct this, the AEG Schnellbahn AG (AEG Rapid Transit Company) was formed, but in 1912 half the shares in this company were acquired by the municipality for a payment of 5.9 million Mark. The municipal authorities also guaranteed the remainder of the capital.

Construction began in 1913 but had not proceeded very far when war broke out and the work was suspended. The AEG Schnellbahn AG went into liquidation during the period of inflation and the works, as far as they then existed, passed to the control of the City. In turn, the municipality passed these to the Nordsüdbahn AG, with the remit of completing and opening the line for service. Work was resumed after the currency had been stabilised and the first section was opened for traffic on 17 July 1927, running between Boddinstrasse and Schönleinstrasse. Heading north from the latter, Kottbusser Tor was reached on 12 February 1928 and Neanderstrasse (now Heinrich-Heine-Strasse) on 6 April 1928. The final extension southwards took place from Boddinstrasse to Leinestrasse on 4 August 1929 and northwards from Neanderstrasse to Gesundbrunnen on 18 April 1930.

Line D, then 9.65 km long, offered interchange with other lines at Alexanderplatz (AI & AII), Kottbusser Tor (BI & BII, where the narrow profile lines' high-level station was resited for interchange purposes) and Hermannplatz (CII).

The last new U-Bahn line to be built prior to the Second World War (and, as it turned out, for 26 years) was line E, opened on 21 December 1930 between Alexanderplatz and Friedrichsfelde, with a depot at the latter. Also built wholly underground, the line was 7.1 km long and comprised ten stations in total. At the eastern end of Alexanderplatz can be seen the alignment of a proposed line to Weissensee. Only Alexanderplatz had interchange with other U-Bahn lines (AI, AII and D).

The reinstatement of services on the large profile lines, after the Second World War, is summarised below and opposite, again using the present day line numbers. Shuttle services are indicated by an asterisk.

Date	Sections Reopened/Operated
Line U5	
16.06.45	*Petersburger Strasse (Rathaus Friedrichshain)–Friedrichsfelde
20.06.45	Schillingstrasse–Petersburger Strasse (*actually a shuttle Schillingstrasse–Friedrichsfelde
23.06.45	Alexanderplatz–Schilingstrasse (*actually a shuttle Alexanderplatz–Friedrichsfelde)
25.09.45	*Shuttles in operation:
	Alexanderplatz–Memeler Strasse
	Memeler Strasse–Frankfurter Allee
	Frankfurter Allee–Friedrichsfelde
21.10.45	Through services Alexanderplatz–Friedrichsfelde

Date	Sections Reopened/Operated

Lines U6 & U7

Date	Sections Reopened/Operated
14.05.45	*Hermannplatz–Bergstrasse *(Karl-Marx-Strasse)*
09.06.45	*Gardepionierplatz *(Südstern)*–Hermannplatz (with a shuttle service Gardepionierplatz–Bergstrasse)
10.06.45	*Gneisenaustrasse–Gardepionierplatz (shuttle services Gneisenaustrasse–Hermannplatz and Hermannplatz–Bergstrasse)
11.06.45	*Belle-Alliance-Strasse *(Mehringdamm)*–Tempelhof (Südring)
11.06.45	*Belle-Alliance-Strasse–Gneisenaustrasse (shuttles Belle-Alliance-Strasse–Hermannplatz and Hermannplatz–Bergstrasse)
26.06.45	Belle-Alliance-Strasse–Bergstrasse (replacing shuttles Belle-Alliance-Strasse–Hermannplatz and Hermannplatz–Bergstrasse)
04.07.45	*Hallesches Tor–Belle-Alliance-Strasse
12.07.45	*Seestrasse–Schwartzkopffstrasse
12.07.45	*Schwartzkopffstrasse–Bahnhof Friedrichstrasse
12.07.45	*Bahnhof Friedrichstrasse–Kochstrasse
26.07.45	*Bergstrasse–Grenzallee
29.07.45	Belle-Alliance-Strasse–Flughafen *(Platz der Luftbrücke)*, with section Flughafen–Tempelhof (Südring) closed
15.09.45	Kochstrasse–Hallesches Tor reopened with through service Seestrasse–Bergstrasse, replacing four shuttles: Seestrasse–Schwartzkopffstrasse, Schwartzkopffstrasse–Bahnhof Friedrichstrasse, Bahnhof Friedrichstrasse–Kochstrasse and Hallesches Tor–Belle-Alliance-Strasse. The shuttle Belle-Alliance-Strasse–Flughafen closed, no rolling stock available
05.12.45	Through service Seestrasse–Grenzallee and shuttle Grenzallee–Bergstrasse.
01.02.46	*Franz-Mehring-Strasse *(was Belle-Alliance-Strasse, now Mehringdamm)*–Tempelhof (Südring)
22.02.47	*Franz-Mehring-Strasse–Tempelhof (Südring) closed to save current
13.03.47	*Franz-Mehring-Strasse–Tempelhof (Südring)
19.05.47	Franz-Mehring-Strasse–Tempelhof (Südring) double-tracked

Line U8

Date	Sections Reopened/Operated
14.05.45	*Schönleinstrasse–Boddinstrasse
17.05.45	*Hermannplatz–Leinestrasse
21.05.45	Schönleinstrasse–Leinestrasse (through services)
22.05.45	*Gesundbrunnen–Rosenthaler Platz
27.05.45	*Kottbusser Tor–Schönleinstrasse
03.06.45	*Neanderstrasse *(Heinrich-Heine-Strasse)*–Kottbusser Tor
13.06.45	*Rosenthaler Platz–Weinmeisterstrasse
16.06.45	Weinmeisterstrasse–Neanderstrasse (with a through service resumed between Gesundbrunnen and Leinestrasse)

It was not until 1953 that construction work for new lines and extensions restarted, after the currency reform and Blockade, under the then governing Mayor of West Berlin, Ernst Reuter, when a number of new projects were launched. Construction began that year of a northern extension to lines CI and CII, the first stage from Seestrasse to Kurt-Schumacher-Platz opening on 3 May 1956. A further extension opened on 31 May 1958 and took CI/II further north to Tegel *(now Alt-Tegel)*, three stations of which (Scharnweberstrasse, Seidelstrasse and Holzhauser Strasse) were in the open air. Although probably regarded as being 'modern' at the time, these three stations of concrete build now look a little austere and certainly dated, especially compared with West Berlin U-Bahn stations built from the 1970s onwards.

Hot on the heels of line C's extension, construction began in 1955 of a new north-south route, line G, 7.1 km long between Leopoldplatz and Spichernstrasse, considerably west of north-south lines C and D. As mentioned hitherto, the construction of this line necessitated line BII closing from 18 November 1957 until 2 September 1961, although it gained a new station (interchanging with line G) at Kurfürstendamm, as well as the reconstruction and resiting of stations on line AII, and interchange with it at Spichernstrasse. Line G also provided interchange with CI/CII at Leopoldplatz and AI at Zoologischer Garten. Line G was opened for passenger service on 28 August 1961, just 15 days after the complete separation of East and West Berlin by the Wall. Immediately it provided an important north-south link, avoiding East Berlin.

We have already seen the effect the Wall had on the small profile lines and now we must consider the large profile routes, although it must be said that this was less serious. Line E, wholly in East Berlin, came under the management of BVG (East). Lines CI/CII and D, although West Berlin lines, had some intermediate stations in East Berlin and from 13 August 1961 these were closed and sealed, trains subsequently running through non-stop. On lines CI and CII the stations were Walter-Ulbricht-Stadion *(originally and now Schwartzkopffstrasse),* Nordbahnhof *(now Zinnowitzer Strasse),* Oranienburger Tor, Französische Strasse and Stadtmitte. This last-named station in fact remained partially open and continued to serve the northern section of line A, wholly in East Berlin. Friedrichstrasse station remained open as the border crossing point between East and West. On line D, the stations that were closed and non-stopped were Bernauer Strasse, Rosenthaler Platz, Weinmeisterstrasse, Alexanderplatz (lines A and E completely in East Berlin remained open here), Jannowitzbrücke and Heinrich-Heine-Strasse *(originally named Neanderstrasse).*

With the building of the Wall, a (successful) boycott of the West Berlin S-Bahn system ensued, with most of its passengers choosing to use longer and more circuitous routes, and often by bus. Expansion of the U-Bahn in West Berlin continued apace and new lines were planned with the presence of the Wall in mind. Meanwhile, line CII was extended further south-east from Grenzallee to Britz-Süd on 28 September 1963, which was to become part of the new all-underground line H between Mehringdamm *(originally Belle-Alliance-Strasse)* and Britz-Süd, leaving the Mehringdamm–Tempelhof section to be served by all trains to and from Tegel. This division of lines was achieved on 28 February 1966 and from the same date, the first brand new section of line H was opened from Mehringdamm to Möckernbrücke, offering interchange with line A at the latter, with services on this 'new' line then operating between Möckernbrücke and Britz-Süd. On the same date, a new extension was also opened on line C, southwards from Tempelhof to Alt-Mariendorf. The following day, 1 March 1966, all U-Bahn lines in West Berlin were numbered, prefixed by the letter 'U', the large profile lines becoming as follows:

U6	Tegel *(now Alt-Tegel)*–Alt-Mariendorf	U8	Gesundbrunnen–Leinestrasse
U7	Möckernbrücke–Britz-Süd	U9	Leopoldplatz–Spichernstrasse

Platform lengthening at Friedrichstrasse nearing completion in September 1995. *Capital Transport*

Although no more extensions are planned for line U6, the stations on this line in former East Berlin are being lengthened – at present these preclude trains longer than four cars being operated. Completed are Französische Strasse, Friedrichstrasse and Oranienburger Tor, with work in progress at Schwartzkopffstrasse, Zinnowitzer Strasse and Stadtmitte. It is planned that six-car trains will be introduced on line U6 for the winter 1996 schedules.

For lines U7, U8 and U9 however, extensions were planned for all three.

Line U7 ventured further into the south-east suburbs, reaching Zwickauer Damm from Britz-Süd on 2 January 1970 and the ultimate destination, Rudow, on 1 July 1972. Despite being an outer suburban terminal station, Rudow ranks as the U-Bahn's busiest station, because of the large residential area it serves and its close proximity to Schönefeld Airport.

Line U9 meanwhile was extended five stations south from Spichernstrasse to Walther-Schreiber-Platz on 29 January 1971 and on the same day U7 was extended seven stations westwards from Möckernbrücke to Fehrbelliner Platz. This latter extension provided three U-Bahn interchanges – with U4 at Bayerischer Platz, U9 at Berliner Strasse and U1 at Fehrbelliner Platz.

In East Berlin, line E had a modest one-station extension realised on 25 June 1973, from Friedrichsfelde to Tierpark.

Priority in West Berlin was then given to line U9, with a southern two-station extension from Walther-Schreiber-Platz to Rathaus Steglitz opening on 30 September 1974, and north-eastwards from Leopoldplatz to Osloer Strasse on 30 April 1976. This latter extension made U9 its present configuration and a length of 12.52 km. Line U8 also gained a two-station extension north-westwards on 5 October 1977, from Gesund-brunnen to Osloer Strasse, enabling interchange with line U9 at its terminus.

Construction north-west of line U7 continued unabated, however, and the final three stages opened has made it operationally the longest of all the U-Bahn lines at 31.70 km – and all underground. The first of three took it northwards from Fehrbelliner Platz to Richard-Wagner-Platz on 28 April 1978 which it replaced, after a long period of closure, the shuttle line of U5 that closed in 1970. The new link in fact served the new station at Bismarckstrasse on U1, rather than hitherto at Deutsche Oper (which itself was originally called Bismarckstrasse). Line U7 then proceeded north and then westwards, reaching Rohrdamm on 1 October 1980 and finally Rathaus Spandau exactly four years later. This line ran through the huge Siemens industrial complex and several stations on the line of route served it. The stations on this route, especially the last-opened section, can only be described as opulent, reflecting the finance available and the grand scale of investment for such projects.

Readers may be wondering what happened to a proposed line F, latterly line U10 (between Drakestrasse in the south-west and Weissensee in the north-east), which has so far been missing from the story. Quite simply it has not been built, although provision was made for it at two stations on line U9 at which interchange was proposed. At Rathaus Steglitz, line U9 uses the platforms proposed for line F, its own platforms being complete but unused as yet. Schloss-Strasse, one station away, has two island platforms, of which one face in each direction are used by U9, while the other two faces are reserved for line U10, complete with track but no current rails. In present proposals, however, it seems that the plans for line U10 have been laid to rest, presumably as it was to serve 'East' and 'West' when the Wall was in situ. Two other stations on the proposed line U10 have been built deep underground and far away from the public eye. These are at Kleistpark and Innsbrucker Platz, the latter being constructed at the same time in the 1960s as the urban motorway through the area.

A similar situation exists with unused platforms on line U7 at Jungfernheide, which also has two island platforms, with one face in each direction being reserved for the (long-term) extension of the present line U5, of which, more below. At Rathaus Spandau, the two outer faces of the two island platforms there await a long-term extension of the present line U2 from Ruhleben. These as yet unused platforms at Jungfernheide and Rathaus Spandau are protected by barriers and are devoid of track.

A more detailed summary of the aborted U-Bahn proposals follows later.

Friedrich-Wilhelm-Platz is typical of the under-ground stations built in West Berlin in the 1960s and in the early 1970s – plain and functional.
Brian Hardy

The grandeur of station decor was also applied to the northern extension of line U8, north from Osloer Strasse to Paracelsus-Bad, with three new stations opening on 27 April 1987. Not only has consideration of station design being taken into account, but also passenger comfort, in 'air-conditioning'. Your writer, visiting Berlin in the summer of 1994, was amazed and pleasantly surprised at the coolness of the stations on this section, when temperatures outside were up to 34°C. A further four stations were added to the northern section of U8 from 24 September 1994, when the line reached Wittenau, giving interchange with S-Bahn lines S1 and S2 at the terminus. Also under construction at present on line U8 is a southern extension from Leinestrasse to Hermannstrasse, primarily to provide interchange with the recently reopened S-Bahn 'Ring' line.

We must now return to East Berlin in the 1980s. Apart from the aforementioned one-station extension from Fredrichsfelde to Tierpark in 1973, the operation of large profile line E remained largely unchanged for a further 15 years. However, new urban development was occurring in East Berlin. To serve these, new lines were provided and the original intention was to wholly develop the East Berlin S-Bahn network. However, another new line to feed into the centre of East Berlin was deemed as saturating the existing system and the simpler and less costly option was to extend U-Bahn line E beyond Tierpark into the eastern suburbs to serve the new housing developments. At Tierpark, the line was facing south-east and to serve the intended area it had to turn almost 90 degrees to head in a north-east direction. Apart from a short section beyond Tierpark and between the new stations of Wuhletal and Kaulsdorf Nord, the line was constructed in the open. Opened on 1 July 1988, the line reached Elsterwerdaer Platz and exactly a year later, was extended to Hönow. Cross-platform interchange was provided at Wuhletal with what became S-Bahn line S5, while between Paul-Verner-Strasse *(now Louis-Lewin-Strasse),* and Hönow, extensive open-air carriage stabling sidings were provided on the south side of the line. Because of the urban nature of this extension, reversing facilities for some trains was built at Biesdorf-Süd, where alternate trains (Monday to Friday midday off-peak) short work to here from Alexanderplatz.

The opening of the border between East and West Berlin occurred on 9 November 1989. Almost immediately, travel between the East and West became more relaxed and subsequently unrestricted. The implications for the small profile lines has already been described, but for lines U6 and U8, it was simply a case of reopening closed stations, although this was easier said than done! It was possible, however, for Jannowitzbrücke to reopen just two days later, on 11 November 1989, followed by Rosenthaler Platz on 22 December 1989 and Bernauer Strasse on 12 April 1990 – all on line U8. Other closed stations took a little longer to reopen and this occurred on the date of reunification – 1 July 1990. These were as follows:

Line U6	Line U8
Stadion der Weltjugend *	Weinmeisterstrasse
Nordbahnhof *	Alexanderplatz §
Oranienburger Tor	Heinrich-Heine-Strasse
Französische Strasse	
Stadtmitte §	

* Stadion der Weltjugend was renamed from Schwartzkopffstrasse in 1973 whilst closed and reverted to Schwartzkopffstrasse in 1991 after it had reopened. Nordbahnhof *(originally Stettiner Bahnhof)* was renamed Zinnowitzer Strasse in 1991.

§ Alexanderplatz on East Berlin lines A and E always remained open, as did Stadtmitte on line A.

Former East Berlin line E was absorbed into the numbering and 'U' prefix system, used in West Berlin since 1 March 1966, and used the gap created by the closure of small profile shuttle line between Deutsche Oper and Richard-Wagner-Platz in May 1970 – U5.

At the forefront of the BVG's U-Bahn expansion and extension programme is that for U5, ultimately to serve Tegel Airport. From Alexanderplatz, the line will run westwards 4.2 km to Lehrter Stadtbahnhof and then via Jungfernheide (q.v. above) to Tegel Airport. Construction of the first 4.2 km is to take place over a seven-year period with completion scheduled in 2002. It is being built in the direction from west to east and therefore it will have to open at once rather than in stages. There will be intermediate stations at Berlin City Hall, Spreeinsel, Unter den Linden, Brandenburger Tor and Reichstag (all of which are subject to different names). The cost of this first stage will be DEM 213 milliard.

Among other routes under consideration for the long-term future are U7 from Rudow to Schönefeld Airport and from Rathaus Spandau to Staaken, and U9 southwards to Lankwitz. All of these plans, of course, including those mentioned for the small profile lines, depend on finance being available and committed over a 35-year period of development.

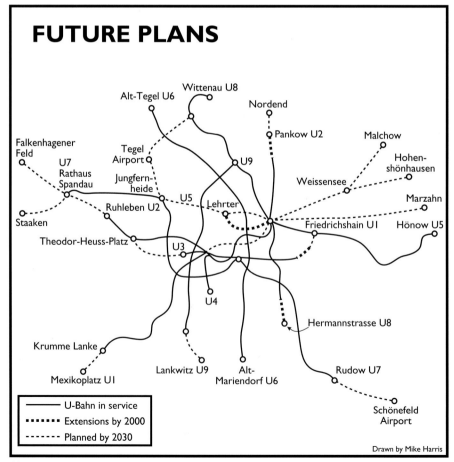

FUTURE PLANS

Drawn by Mike Harris

With the extension of Large Profile U5 to Hönow in 1989, cross-platform interchange was arranged at Wuhletal with S-Bahn line S5. A class E3/5 train proceeds east to Hönow (left) while a class 485 train proceeds east on line S5 (right) on 28 June 1993. The class E type of stock, mostly converted from older S-Bahn vehicles, are now but a memory. *Steve Williams*

A train of DL.68 stock on U5 heads an Alexanderplatz train on line U5 into Wuhletal, having passed under the inbound track of line S5. *Brian Hardy*

Unfulfilled Plans

To a greater extent than other cities, perhaps, Berlin has a history of unfulfilled plans for extensions to its underground railways.

The first interruption to the programme came with the outbreak of war in 1914, but for which a number of extensions and new lines would have been built. The little branch to Uhlandstrasse would have been extended along the Kurfürstendamm, then south to Halensee and south west to a terminus in the area of Grunewald. From Wilhelmplatz, a branch would have run north, then west, to Spandau and from the first station on this extension, in Moabit, a new large profile line would have run east to Lehrter Bahnhof, south to Potsdamer Platz, east along the line of Leipziger Strasse and then south east to terminate in Treptow. This line would have served Görlitzer Bahnhof, which was rather out on a limb. Schöneberg had plans for a three-station extension of its line in the direction of Steglitz. Finally, a new line (it is not clear to what profile) would have started at Wittenbergplatz and gone by way of Anhalter Bahnhof and Alexanderplatz towards Weissensee.

While the NS government did nothing at all for the U-Bahn, it did produce some grandiose plans for extensions, in keeping with the development of the capital of the "thousand-year empire". The most modest was that for an extension of line A in Pankow, the extension of which is now under construction – many years later. Line B would have been extended at its eastern end northwards to connect with the new line F1 at a station names Thaerstrasse, having interchange with line E en route. At its other end, line B would have taken the Uhlandstrasse branch along the Kurfürstendamm, as in the 1914 plans, but then turned directly southwards to cross line A at Dahlem Dorf and terminate at Lichterfelde West. Line C would have been extended south to the racecourse (Trabrennbahn) at Mariendorf, just slightly beyond the point it did reach in 1966, while its northern terminus would have been one station beyond Seestrasse, at Otawistrasse, again on the line of the modern extension. However, line C would have lost the branch from Belle-Alliance-Strasse *(now Mehringdamm)* to Grenzallee, which would have formed part of a new line H (q.v.). Line D would have had a two-station extension northwards from Gesundbrunnen to Christianiastrasse and a southern extension to Britz.

Although line U15 to Uhlandstrasse is extended to Warschauer Strasse for the main part of the day on Mondays to Saturdays, it continues to operate as a shuttle to and from Wittenbergplatz evenings and Sundays. One such train is seen on the left, beside a train on line U1. Things would have been different here if the 1914 plans had come into being. *Brian Hardy*

The present terminus of line U9 at Rathaus Steglitz uses the deep-level platforms intended for the now abandoned line U10, while the upper-level platforms intended for line U9 are as yet unused, as seen on 3 July 1995. *Brian Hardy*

If so far, this programme seems ambitious, it is nothing compared to what was to follow. Line E would have been taken westwards, as is now being done, but would have run north-west from Lehrter Bahnhof to terminate at Beusselstrasse in Moabit. A new line F would have run from Marzahn in the east via Thaerstrasse, Alexanderplatz, Lützowplatz, Zoologischer Garten and Reichskanzlerplatz to Pichelsdorf, from which branches would have reached Spandau in the north (FI) and Kladow in the south (FIII). At Lützowplatz, a branch would have headed south to Wittenbergplatz, where it would have been picked up the Schöneberg line and extended this, as FII, by five stations to Lankwitz.

Line G would have been a relief line to C, running west of it from Marienfelde in the south to Lübars in the north via Kemperplatz, Invalidenstrasse and Seestrasse. New line H would have begun at a station in the area of Gleisdreieck and run to Belle-Alliance-Strasse where it would have picked up the branch of line C and followed it to Grenzallee, with a one-station extension to Buschkrug, almost as opened in 1963. Finally, there would have been a U-Bahn ring, built within the S-Bahn Ringbahn. Starting in a clockwise direction from Deutsche Oper, its course would have lain north then west through Moabit to Invalidenstrasse and on to Stettiner Bahnhof. From there it would have run to the north of Alexanderplatz then south-east to Warschauer Brücke, where it would have joined line B to the now closed station of Osthafen. Leaving that, it would have gone south to Rathaus Neukölln, then turned west to Boddinstrasse and on to Flughafen (Platz der Luftbrücke). Continuing west, it would have intersected the Schöneberg line at Bayerischer Platz and line AII at Fehrbelliner Platz before turning north via Wilmersdorfer Strasse to its starting point. Certain lines in the area of Gleisdreieck would, in conjunction with the opening of new lines, be closed to traffic.

The whole system would have been immensely complicated and it may be that the proposals were intended more as propaganda than as serious planning. Nonetheless, some work was started at various sites in 1939, only to be abandoned in the following year.

In no way dismayed by the lack of success of pre-war plans, the senate of West Berlin produced in 1955 the first version of what was to become known as the 200 km plan. Despite the growing division of the city, it was based on the assumption that there would one day be a re-unified transport network. This plan underwent various changes over the years, as political events unfolded, but it did have some successes, such as the northern extension of line U8. The revitalisation of the S-Bahn in the west after 1984, the development of modern tramways in the east, and above all reunification, all altered the original basis of the plan and it is now doubtful if all its proposals will become reality. Unfulfilled proposals were as follows, the line numbers referring to those in use in 1989:

Line 1: Originally this would have been extended at its eastern end only, to intersect line E at Frankfurter Tor. As this section has since been covered by a tram line largely rebuilt on reserved track, it has been dropped from the plan. The western terminus at first remained at Ruhleben but by 1977 it was proposed to extend the line via Rathaus Spandau to Falkenhagener Feld. The future reopening of the S-Bahn line to Spandau now makes this unlikely.

Line 2: In Pankow this would have been extended by two stations, rather than one, as is now being done, to meet an extended line U9 at Breite Strasse. In the south, it would have been extended beyond Krumme Lanke to meet the S-Bahn at Lindenthaler Allee (the present Mexikoplatz) and on beyond this to Düppel.

Line 3: Based on the pre-war plan, this would have been extended to Pichelsdorf, along the line of the proposed line F, then north to Hakenfelde. By 1984, the proposals had been curtailed to an extension along the Kurfürstendamm to Theodor-Heuss-Platz and a possible link to line U4, which was not in itself to be altered in any way.

Line E: This line was marked '5' in the plan (and which number the present line took). The original eastward extension was to be Karlshorst and Oberschöneweide but this was later changed to the plan that was realised in 1989. In the west, the line would have been taken via Unter den Linden (as is now happening) and on via Turmstrasse and Jungfernheide to Flughafen Tegel.

Line 7: At its western end this line would have been prolonged beyond Spandau to Falkenhagener Feld. When it was decided to serve this section by line U1, line 7 would then have run south-west to Staaken.

Line 8: In the south this line would be extended to Britz. An extension to Hermann-strasse is now being built.

Line 9: In the north this line would be prolonged to meet line U2 at Breite Strasse while in the south it would have run beyond Rathaus Steglitz to Marienfelde via Lankwitz. The likely reintroduction of trams to the western part of the city will obviate the need for the former proposal, while the revival of the S-Bahn has already made the latter superfluous.

Line 10: Post-war, this was also referred to as line F. This was essentially the Weissensee line of pre-1914 plans and line FII of 1939. It was to run from Weissensee to Alexanderplatz, then via the old city centre, with a station at Schloss-Strasse, to Potsdamer Platz, south to Kleistpark, south-west to Rathaus Steglitz and on in the same direction to terminate at Lichterfelde, Drakestrasse. The revival of the S-bahn in the south and the improvement of tramways in the north have now removed much of the need for this line. However, some parts of the infrastructure for it, such as unused platforms as previously described, were built with other civil engineering works.

Quite separate from the 200 km plan, BVB later proposed three extensions in its area. These would have run from the inner area to Marzahn, from Leninallee to Hohenschönhausen and from Tierpark to Weissensee. All have since been covered by tram routes rebuilt to light rail standards.

Ghost Stations and the "Special Sections"

The construction of the Berlin Wall in 1961 brought considerable operational difficulties for the sections of U-Bahn lines which passed beneath the eastern part of the city. Lines U6 and U8 were affected, the former being more important in terms of passenger numbers. On 13 August 1961, four stations on U6 and six stations on U8 were closed to passengers, but while U8 could then run non-stop under the eastern section, trains on U6 continued to stop at Friedrichstrasse, where interchange with the western S-Bahn lines could be made without passing through the DDR entry procedures. Four stations on the Nord-Süd S-Bahn were likewise closed.

Stations which lay directly on the sector boundary – Stadion der Weltjugend, Stadtmitte (platforms on U6 only), Bernauer Strasse and Heinrich-Heine-Strasse, were guarded by DDR frontier troops, the others by DDR transport police. Until June 1965, train dispatchers continued to occupy their normal position on the platforms, although there were no trains to dispatch! For the station guards, bunkers were constructed with observation slits at a height which allowed watch to be kept from a seated position, although from time to time they would also patrol the platforms, on which lighting had been reduced to the bare minimum. The bunkers could be closed off from the platform. On some track diagrams, direction was indicated as "Freundwarts" (To friends) and "Fiendwarts" (To the enemy).

There was a central control post, with alarms, at Friedrichstrasse, where there was also a model of that station used in the long and intensive training of frontier guards. Trains passed through the "ghost stations" as Berliners soon nicknamed the closed stations, at a maximum speed of 25 kph (30 kph on the S-Bahn).

Jannowitzbrücke on line U8 was the first U-Bahn station to reopen after the opening of the west/east frontier on 9 November 1989 – just two days later. *Nick Agnew*

For a visitor, it was an eerie experience to travel on one of these sections, having been forewarned by a gloomy voice at stations such as Kochstrasse, "Letzter Bahnhof in West Berlin" ("last station in West Berlin"). As the train crawled through the twilight of the first ghost station, there might be a glimpse of the armed guards patrolling the platform before normal speed was resumed. Most times, however, there was nothing to see and Berliners normally did not bother to look up from their newspapers. The job of the guards must have been incredibly boring.

The station facilities were left almost exactly as they had been on the night of 12/13 August 1961, even to litter and advertisements, which remained untouched until early in 1990. In a few places, openings in walls were made to allow better sight lines, and the escalators at Potsdamer Platz (S-Bahn) were removed for the same reason. Certain items, such as destination indicators, were removed over the years, but generally everything was left to moulder into decay and by 1990 the stations presented a sorry sight. Above ground, station entrances were blocked off with concrete and all signs were removed – after 25 years it was difficult to tell where these had once been, if one did not know where to look.

Of all the stations affected, Friedrichstrasse was probably the oddest. On the underground platforms, the DDR authorities set up Intershops, where duty-free goods were sold at prices much lower than those in the west – after all, it was a frontier post! At first these sold tobacco, alcohol and confectionery but later the range was expanded to include perfume, toys and records, the last of these often being very good and a great bargain. These shops drew so much business from West Berliners that the platform became known as "Kaufhaus Friedrichstrasse" ("Friedrichstrasse Department Store"). Of course there was always a chance of western customs officers boarding the train at the first station in the west and some passengers went to considerable lengths to conceal their purchases, using different packaging or hiding them about their person – the words "stocking filler" took on a different meaning!

The platforms concerned were patrolled by the frontier police, usually in threes, these being under orders not to approach trains which were stopped in the station. Generally these were tall, smartly-uniformed young men, whose speech often betrayed their Saxon origin and gave rise to the rumour that the DDR authorities could not trust Berliners to do the job properly. In fairness, it should be said that the DDR frontier officials were generally extremely polite to visitors from outside Germany and often positively welcoming – and it was a good idea to remember that they had all the time in the world!

Operationally, the problem of running underground trains under the territory of another country, with which, for much of the time, one's government was not on speaking terms, called for technical ingenuity, a cool head and considerable tact. All trains had to be manned by a crew of two for the transit and certain unlucky individuals spent their entire shift shuttling between the first and last western stations. The only task they actually performed was to signal the train away from Friedrichstrasse if there was no DDR dispatcher on the platform. This was indicated by an additional signal, as necessary. At times such as holidays, where many people were making for "over there", serious overcrowding often occurred on U6 since the platforms at Friedrichstrasse (and also the closed stations) were only 85 metres long, and trains were limited to four coaches. On line U8, however, six coach trains could be operated, but traffic levels justified only the running of four coach sets in peak hours and two-car sets at other times.

To enable a service to be operated in the separate parts of West Berlin served by these lines, in the event that the transit section had to be closed, additional crossings were installed at stations such as Reinickendorfer Strasse on U6. New sidings were also brought into use at certain stations just within West Berlin. Along with the lengthening of platforms in western stations, these allowed the operation of six-coach trains on shuttle services north and south of the eastern section. In other respects, these lines remained technically in the condition of 1961, with mechanical trainstops (necessitating the equipping of all large profile trains with both these and magnetic stops) and an electrical supply system which gradually crumbled into total unreliability.

If matters were difficult enough under 'normal' conditions, breakdowns posed a much greater problem. As all of the installations gradually came to be in more and more need of renewal, these happened with increasing frequency as the years progressed. Cab radio could not be used in these sections in the event of a failure of a train and rescue could be initiated only after the eastern authorities had telephoned BVG to report a stalled train. An answer to a question in the Senate of West Berlin gave the information that, in the years from 1973 to 1981, there were 24 such failures and, while most led only to a short wait in the train, some brought longer delays. An example of this occurred on 1 November 1975, when a train on U8 broke down just inside Bernauer Strasse station, and passengers had to endure its cold platforms for some 2½ hours before being rescued. An increased number of failures in 1981 led to an agreement that trains could be rescued by a BVG diesel locomotive and this led to a reduction in the delays to passengers.

On the S-Bahn the action laid down in the rules provided that passengers from a stalled train should be walked back through the tunnel to the next station, where they would be put on a train going in the opposite direction, or taken above ground and put on a bus to Friedrichstrasse. On one occasion, the passengers were brought to the surface before the bus arrived and they were temporarily incarcerated in a nearby bookshop, where they no doubt made use of the time brushing up on Marxism! Some emergency exits were retained on both the U- and S-Bahn, but in many cases these were restricted and it would have been very difficult to evacuate an entire trainload through them in the event of a real emergency.

There was, of course, no physical barrier at the sector boundary underground, simply a white stripe, a shutter which rolled back into the tunnel roof and a notice "Achtung, Zonengrenze" ("Attention, zone boundary"). An alarm signal in the guards' quarters in the nearest station and, later, lights, would have given away anyone who tried to reach the west via one of the tunnels. In practice, there was no need for these – it was almost impossible for any member of the public to gain access to the tunnels and for staff, the feeling that one was being closely watched at all times and the inability to tell who was doing the watching, prevented any attempt to use the tunnels as an escape route to the west.

It says a great deal for the professionalism of Berlin's railway staff, on both sides, that this "system" was made to work for some 28 years with only minimal inconvenience to the travelling public. And, as a six-coach train on U6 pulls into the lengthened, well-lit station of Französische Strasse, it is now hard to remember how different things were not very long ago.

The M-Bahn

The concept of the M-Bahn, a train powered by linear induction motors and suspended on a magnetic field, was developed from 1973 by the firm Magnetbahn GmbH of Braunschweig, with, from 1978, the support of AEG. In 1982, the Senate of West Berlin, with support from the BMFT, decided to build a test track for the system, using part of the trackbed of line U2 from Gleisdreieck station to just north of the Landwehrkanal, a distance of 535.5 metres. From there, the test track would leave the abandoned trackbed and swing westwards into a new station at Bernburger Strasse. Leaving this, the line would cross what had been the area of Potsdamer Bahnhof to terminate at the station of Kemperplatz, near the Philharmonie concert hall. This second stretch would be 927.2 m long. The line would serve both as a demonstration track and would also fill one of the gaps in the U-Bahn network, being worked as part of the latter.

Work on the alteration of Gleisdreieck station began in June 1983 and on the other two stations on 26 September 1986, by which date the track had been laid. Bernberger Strasse was laid out with two side platforms and to gain sufficient room for this, the street of the same name had to be diverted slightly to the south. Work on fitting doors to the platform at Gleisdreieck began in January 1987.

The cost, originally given at DEM 50-million, had by 1986 risen to DEM 88-million and in that year a further increase of DEM 7-million was announced. There were also protests at the likely effect on the environment and in December 1985 work on the construction was halted for one week.

The first vehicle to appear was a works car, which was diesel powered and had no magnetic drive or linear power. It was numbered 05 and was delivered in March 1984, being removed in March 1986 having served its purpose in the construction. The first passenger car arrived in June 1984. It was numbered 706 and made its first demonstration run on 26 June. Test running began the following month. The first two cars intended for the line were delivered in October and November 1986 and began trial running in March 1987. The bodywork was by Waggon-Union, the underframe by Magnetbahn GmbH and the drive by AEG. They were numbered 01 and 02 of class M80/2.

The service was planned to start on 1 May 1987, to coincide with the celebrations for Berlin's 750th anniversary. In the event, it proved impossible to keep to this date and a starting date of 1 September was announced. However, early in the morning of 18 April a fire broke out at Gleisdreieck and caused damage worth DEM 5-million before it could be extinguished. Car 01 was totally destroyed and car 02 was severely damaged. At the end of the year, another starting date was published – March 1988. Service was to be a shuttle using cars 03 and 04. Car 02 had to be returned to the Magnetbahn, where it was rebuilt to be used as a model demonstration vehicle. In the meantime, costs had soared to DEM 145-million. Of this the BMFT and the Senate of West Berlin paid DEM 88.5-million, the Magnetbahn Company DEM 45-million. It was not clear how the balance was to be made up.

The announced starting date came and went and still there was no public service. Then on 19 December 1988, disaster struck again. A test train made up of cars 03 and 04 failed to stop at Kemperplatz and went through the end wall of the station. Fortunately, no one was injured but car 03 was so badly damaged that it had to be removed. Finally, a free public service began on 28 August 1989, using cars 04 and 06 as a two-car shuttle and over 25,000 passengers sampled what the posters proclaimed to be "Ein Erlebnis" (an experience) in the first four days of operation. This period of service ended on 5 October to allow work to proceed on the installation of car 07, but was resumed immediately and lasted until 22 December. There was then another break until 3 January 1990, by which date, of course, transport planning had begun to change. Finally, this period of running came to an end on 17 September 1990, by which date 1.7-million passengers had been carried. However, in January of that year, the Senate had already sealed the fate of the line by announcing that it would be dismantled in 1992, to permit work to begin on rebuilding line U2. Despite this decision, services resumed on 11 January 1991.

All this time, service had been free, permission to operate as a public carrier not having been received. This was finally granted on 18 July 1991 and for the last two weeks of its life, the M-Bahn was run as a normal part of BVG operations, ticket machines and cancellers being installed at stations. Passenger service ended at 22.45 on 31 July 1991, though decommissioning runs continued until 16 September. Work on the demolition of the line began the next day. The eventual cost of this was DEM 11-million.

In some respects, the short history of the M-Bahn reads like a Greek tragedy, with Fate ever ready to deal a blow, just when it seemed that matters were beginning to go right. But in reality, it seemed to serve little purpose – it was a technical and political toy, supported to show that West Berlin could still pioneer new concepts, at a time when it was difficult to attract investment to the area and there was a danger that the city could be sinking slowly into subsidised nostalgia. Once support had begun, it became a case of throwing good money after bad, to keep the project afloat. The total cost has not been published, but the BMFT and the Senate did invest DEM 88-million and it was thought that AEG put DEM 150-million into the venture. At current prices, this amount could have bought over 100 new trams!

In service, the trains appeared to rise vertically before they moved forward. They were rather cramped with little to distinguish them from a narrow profile U-Bahn car, and the speed was sedate. But perhaps the line did not have a real chance to prove itself – genuine public service lasted for only two weeks and its fate had already been sealed by then, giving no chance for it to show how it could fit into Berlin's transport pattern.

M-Bahn Rolling Stock

No.	Type	Builder	In Service	Disposal
706	M70/2	MBB	Jun-84	Removed Oct-86
01	M80/2	WU	Mar-87	Scrapped Dec-87
02	M80/2	WU	Mar-87	Removed Feb-88
03	M80/2	WU	May-87	Removed Jul-89
04	M80/2	WU	May-87	Removed Sep-91
05	Diesel	MBB	Apr-84	Removed 1986
06	M80/2	WU	Aug-89	Removed Sep-91
07	M80/2	WU	Oct-89	Removed Sep-91

U-Bahn Rolling Stock

Small Profile Stock

The first two prototype cars for the U-Bahn were delivered in 1899 by Von der Zypen and Charlier of Köln. These had two single-width doors at each end and seats were arranged in 2+1 transverse formation. Kaiser Wilhelm II rode in one of these on his first U-Bahn journey in 1908 and they were thereafter referred to as "Kaiserwagen". In service, the seating arrangement restricted passenger movement within the cars and, with the exception of the two experimental trailers in 1929, all later deliveries for the small profile lines had longitudinal seating. Both prototypes were later used in works trains.

For the opening of service in 1902, 42 third class motor cars and 21 second class trailers were assembled in the workshops at Warschauer Brücke. They were designed by the architect Alfred Grenander and were 12.70 metres long and 2.36 metres wide. The bodies were entirely of wood, on a steel underframe. Wooden seats were provided in third class, upholstered seats in second, and a three-car train could accommodate 210 passengers, of whom 122 were seated. Motor cars had three 52kW motors and a maximum speed of 50 km/hr. These cars were later known as class A1.1.

In service, these ran in three-car trains of motor-trailer-motor formation, but it was soon found that this was inadequate and the next batch of motor cars had four motors, to allow operation of four-car trains. Successive deliveries showed no change in the basic design, although the number of side windows varied, but from the fifth series of 1905, electro-magnetic multiple unit equipment was fitted, this being later retrofitted to earlier deliveries. Until 1924, all cars were of wooden construction, but in that year, the first steel trains entered service, with the 16th series. In all, there were 364 motor coaches and 254 trailers of class A1 delivered to the Hochbahn in 18 series.

For its own U-Bahn line, Schöneberg ordered 12 composite motor coaches from MAN. In all other respects these were identical to the stock of the Hochbahn and six further motor cars were delivered in 1912 (some sources give Schöneberg a total of 19 cars).

The closing days of the old narrow profile stock on East Berlin line 'A' in May 1986, now the northern section of line U2. The rear of a train of A1T stock is at Dimitrofstrasse, now named Eberswalder Strasse, but originally named Danziger Strasse. The car, which was originally numbered 259, is of 1924/25 vintage.
Bob Greenaway

Left At the same location is a train in ivory and yellow livery. Note the single hand-worked sliding door and the large number of narrow windows between them. *Bob Greenaway*

Right The A2 type of 1928–29 differed from its A1 predecessors by having double doors, and fewer windows between them. This is at Dimitroffstrasse in 1979. *Brian Patton*

This stock was incorporated into class A1 when it passed to the Hochbahn in 1926 and the 1912-built cars were rebuilt as trailers. Part of one of the motor coaches can be seen on display at the north end of Klosterstrasse station on line U2.

The first new design entered service in 1928, with the delivery of class A2. These had two double-width doors on each side with only three windows in between, and Scharfenberg couplings. Shortly after delivery, one was driven by King Amanullah of Afghanistan, while he was on a state visit to Berlin, and the class was thereafter known as "Amanullah Wagen". Unusually, the number of motors and trailers built was identical, being 96 of each. After these deliveries, new construction of small profile stock ceased for some 30 years.

In service, both classes proved reliable and long-lasting. As recorded elsewhere, 24 each of motors and trailers were fitted with extrusions to allow them to operate safely on new wide profile line C, on which they opened the service in 1923. In this condition, they were nicknamed "Blumenbretter" ("Flower Trays"). When new stock arrived for the line, they were reconverted to their original condition.

Many cars were lost as a result of war damage and eight of class A1 and 11 of class A2 were rebuilt in 1949-51. Many were further rebuilt in 1964-65 for one-person-operation and could thereafter be recognised by full-length end windows. With this came the conversion to air doors – it had long been the habit with certain Berliners to run after a departing train, jump on the step and pull open the doors, and attempts to try this with air doors were dangerous and often fatal. The last trains of class A1 in West Berlin ran on 27 December 1968 on line U1 and the last train of class A2 on 30 April 1973 on U2 (West). The shuttle lines U3 (now U15) and U4 last operated old stock in June 1971. In East Berlin, however, they were to survive for many more years.

Returning now to 1945, many trains of wide profile stock were taken to Moscow as reparations and the BVG (East) found itself with no trains to operate line E. A total of 41 motors and 39 trailers of class A1 were therefore rebuilt with body extrusions to allow them to operate on that line and were once again nicknamed "Blumenbretter" as a result – officially they became class A1.K. When enough S-Bahn trains had been rebuilt for operation on the U-Bahn (q.v. below) the class A1.K were reconverted for the small profile lines and then became class A1.U.

One of the 16 cars of A2 stock at the Nollendorfplatz high level station flea market, being trailer 861. *Alan Blake*

The cab end and part car section of motor coach No.12 from the Schöneberg underground (today's line U4) has been kept for posterity at the north end of Klosterstrasse on line U2. *Bob Greenaway*

At Königs Wusterhausen, adjacent to the S-Bahn and suburban station, a clothing store has been set up in narrow profile cars 512 and 592. They are seen on 3 July 1995. *Jeanne Hardy*

When lines U1/15 were reopened to Warschauer Strasse on 14 October 1995, the Museum train operated on the line. Two views of type A1 stock are seen at Schlesisches Tor on this occasion, the red car denoting 'smoking'.
Dr Volker Wangemann

In 1970, a computer-based numbering system was introduced and the small profile stock became classes 125 (A1 motors), 126 (A1.U motors) and 127 (A2). Trailer cars became classes 175, 176 and 177 respectively. October 1972 proved to be an unlucky month for the old stock, for 14 cars were destroyed in a fire in the sidings at Alexanderplatz on 4 October and another 12 were seriously damaged in a fire in the sidings at Rosa-Luxemburg-Platz a few weeks later. Fortunately, BVG West had trains to spare as a result of the introduction of new stock and BVB acquired 20 motors and 20 trailers of type A2. These became classes 128 and 178 respectively, although three cars were broken up for spares and one motor car was used as a shunter.

With the entry into service of the G1 class in the 1980s, it was clear that the days of the pre-war stock were numbered, but problems with the new trains meant that it was not until 5 November 1989 that the last ran in service. On that day, three trains of A1 and A2 stock were operated, suitably garlanded and carrying special headboards. It was the end of an era which went back to 1902, and some were sorry to see the old trains go, but already change was in the air and most Berliners were too pre-occupied with other events to notice the end of a piece of U-Bahn history. Some of the A class survived as works cars for some time after they ceased to run in passenger service and two four-car sets (one of type A1 and one type A2) have been preserved as Museum trains.

Summary of old Small Profile Stock:

Order No.	Built	Type	Motors	Trailers
1	1901/02	A1	42	21
2	1902	A1	24	9
3	1902/03	A1		4
4	1903/04	A1	-	4
5	1906/07	A1	6	13 *
6	1908	A1	6	8
7	1908	A1	6	-
8	1908	A1	30	28
9	1909	A1	5	-
10	1909	A1	10	10
11	1910	A1	4	4
12	1912	A1	6	11
13	1913	A1	24	24
14	1913	A1	65	36
15	1913	A1	1	-
15	1923/24	A1	-	6
16	1924/25	A1	51	51 §
17	1925/26	A1	12	12
18	1926	A1	72	13
			364	254

Note   * First batch with electro-magnetic multiple unit equipment.
Note   § First steel-built cars.

Order No.	Built	Type	Motors	Trailers
S1	1910	A1	12	-
S2	1912	A1	6	-
			18	

Order No.	Built	Type	Motors	Trailers
19	1928	A2	51	51
20	1928/29	A2	45	45
			96	96

Large Profile Stock

Prototypes

For the proposed north-south line, two prototype cars were ordered from Linke-Hofmann of Breslau and delivered in 1914, when they were tested at the Siemens works. These were 12.5 metres long and 2.65 metres wide and had a capacity for 111 passengers. Accommodation was arranged in five sections with single-width sliding doors to each. As it was planned to use overhead current collection, they were fitted with pantographs. They were later converted to works cars and No.11 survived until 1969.

Two prototypes were also ordered for the AEG-line, from Von der Zypen and Charlier. These arrived in 1916 but could not then be tested and lay idle until 1921, when they were taken over by Deutsche Reichsbahn and put to work on the Lichterfelde line. These cars had clerestory roofs and four single-width doors, the transverse seating being arranged in bays alternating on either side of the car.

Class B

After the currency had been stabilised, new stock was ordered for line C and the first trains entered service in 1924. These were class B1 and from the oval end windows they were known as "Tunneleulen" ("Tunnel Owls") and were, in a way, similar to the 'F' stock on London's District Railway. They were of all steel construction and were rather heavy, at 32.8 tonnes for the motor cars and 19.7 tonnes for the trailers. Dimensions were 13.15 metres long and, of course, 2.65 metres wide. Each motor car had four 85kW motors and Scharfenberg couplings were fitted. Controllers had a dead-man's handle, known as Sifa (Sicherseits Fahrschaltung). In service they operated in trains of three, four or five cars and in all there were 74 motor coaches and 84 trailers.

A much improved version, class B2, was delivered in 1927/28 and of these there were 20 motors and 30 trailers. Due to their superior performance – the motors were of 100kW – the motor cars could not be operated in multiple with class B1.

The "owls" were the mainstay of line C for many years. Many were damaged in 1944/45 and 16 motors and 19 trailers were rebuilt in the period 1947-51. The last ran in service on line U6 on 3 June 1969.

The large profile class B1 stock, of which motor car 35 is an example, is all now operationally a memory. The oval end windows gave these trains the nickname of "Tunneleulen" (tunnel owls). The destination, Hasenheide, is now Südstern on U7, although in the meantime it has also been named Kaiser-Friedrich-Platz (1933–1939) and Gardepionierplatz (1939–1947). The train is seen in the Britz Museum collection in 1983.
Brian Patton

The body of motor car 1193 of class B2 stock currently resides as a ticket box at the entrance for a multivision show inside the Europa centre. Photographed on 27 May 1986, the car was originally numbered 132 and was delivered in 1929. *John Laker*

Class C

It was soon recognised that class B had some shortcomings and that something better was required for the new lines. Accordingly in 1926, the first 18-metre-long cars of class C1 were placed in service and were the subject of prolonged testing in passenger operation. There were 12 each of motors and trailers, while some had three and others had four doors per side. These cars introduced to Berliners the flashing red light which denoted the closing of the doors. Series production of classes C2 and C3 followed in 1929/30 – these had two 100kW motors on the leading bogie and in service operated in motor-motor formation, there being no corresponding trailers. Externally, there was no difference between the two classes, but C2 had air brakes while C3 had electrical braking. The former, of which there were 114, were originally intended for service on line D and the latter, 30 in total, for line E. Finally in 1930, two motor cars and one trailer with aluminium bodywork were delivered, being classified C4. These showed a saving of four tonnes over the steel cars.

No fewer than 120 cars of class C were sent to Moscow as reparations in 1945. These were made up of 12 each of motors from the prototypes, 69 of class C2 and 27 of class C3. In Russia they became classes B1, B2 and B3 respectively – though the equivalent in our alphabet would be 'W' – and the cars in class B1 were rebuilt as trailers. Probably about the end of the 1950s, all cars in class B1 became motors, receiving new Russian equipment and being reclassified B4, while around the same time, 13 cars of class C3 became trailers. In Moscow, the ex-Berlin cars were referred to as a "Special delivery". They were withdrawn in 1965/66 and one continues to exist as a store room in Krasnaja Precnja depot. It is without bogies and has recently been repainted, while the local enthusiasts are trying to get it preserved. Of those that remained, all in West Berlin, the last ran in service on 30 April 1975 on line U8.

Class E

In 1958, two motor coaches of class E1 were delivered to the BVG (East) for service on line E. These were built by VEB Waggonbau Ammendorf and were numbered 1401 and 1402. They were 18 metres long and were clearly derived from class C, having a three-piece windscreen but four doors per side. It was intended that, after trials, series production of what would have been class E2 would have begun. However, the equipment of the prototype cars proved unsatisfactory in service and they did not remain long in traffic. In fact, their unreliability in service resulted in them being nicknamed 'Kaputniks' – in the era of Sputniks!

Given the urgent need to improve services on both lines A and E and the availability of a large number of surplus S-Bahn trains after the building of the Wall in 1961, it was decided not to proceed with the development of class E2. Instead, the rebuilding of the redundant S-Bahn stock as class E3 was put in hand.

In mid-1962 therefore, work began in Schöneweide workshops on the rebuilding of the first of these sets. Following S-Bahn practice, each set comprised a motor and a trailer, each being 17.83 metres long and 2.58 metres wide. In fact, very little of the original cars was used in the rebuilds – only the bogies, motors and control equipment and, in the first series, parts of the underframe were reused – everything else was new. However, the noises produced by these trains in service were completely those of the S-Bahn. The first train entered service on line E between Alexanderplatz and Friedrichsfelde on 1 April 1963. There were in all five series of rebuilds.

Class E3/1 consisted of 22 sets rebuilt from S-Bahn classes ET/EB168 and, for the last three, classes ET/EB165.

Class E3/2 appeared between 1966 and 1968 and numbered 14 sets. In these, the motor cars were rebuilds of class ET169 while the trailers were completely new. With

The E3 trains that operated on line E (now line U5) were mostly conversions from S-Bahn stock, carried out in stages between 1962 and 1990. The first four groups (E3/1 to E3/4) were similar in appearance to each other, this example being an E3/4 class at Biesdorf-Süd. Numbered 1898, it was previously 104.098. *Brian Patton*

The last batch of converted E stock was class E/5 and could be distinguished by their destination blind in the top right hand cab window, as seen on motor 1926 (ex-105.126) leading at Louis-Lewin-Strasse. *Steve Williams*

their entry into service, the last of the small profile stock (the "Blumenbretter" cars) could be removed to line A.

Steadily increasing passenger numbers and the extension to Tierpark required further conversions from 1972 onwards. Class E3/3 was a small group of four trains rebuilt from class ET/EB165.

Class E3/4, in which there were five trains, was converted in 1974/75, at the same time as the modernisation of other S-Bahn sets and the opportunity was taken to incorporate some of the refinements being introduced with this programme. The cars received improved interior decor, a public address system, optical and acoustic door warning and Scharfenberg couplings. The earlier rebuilds were then similarly modernised.

Finally, when the extension to Hönow was planned in the mid-1980s, a further 41 sets were created from what had now become class 275. As these already had modernised electrical equipment they were unable to operate in multiple with previous rebuilds, from which they could be distinguished by the positioning of the destination indicator in the left front window, instead of above the windscreen. The conversion of these took place between 1986 and 1990.

In all, the E3 group of stock comprised 86 motors and 86 trailers, representing 28 six-car trains plus two spare sets. Class E3 were rugged and reliable and certainly helped BVB to improve services quickly at minimal cost, but they could not compete with modern U-Bahn stock. They used more current and were becoming heavy on maintenance. After the merger of the BVB and BVG, it was initially planned to keep some in service until 1999 with a phased withdrawal, but in February 1994 it was decided to withdraw the entire class as soon as possible. The last ran in public service on 8 July 1994, with a farewell trip on 16 July.

Summary of Old Large Profile Stock:

Order No.	Built	Type	Motors	Trailers
1	1924	B1	16	8
2	1924/25	B1	18	26
3	1925	B1	40	40
5	1926	B1	-	10
			74	84

Order No.	Built	Type	Motors	Trailers
8	1927/28	B2	14	21
9	1929	B2	6	9
			20	30

Order No.	Built	Type	Motors	Trailers	Notes
4 & 6	1926/27	C1	12	12	
10	1929/30	C2	114	-	
11	1930	C3	30	-	
7	1930	C4	2	1	*
			158	13	

* Aluminium bodywork.

Rebuilt	Built New	Class	Motors	Trailers (odd)
	1958	E1	1401–1402	
1962–63		E3/1	1802–1844§	1803–1845
1966–68		E3/2	1850–1876§	
	1966–68	E3/2		1851–1877
1972		E3/3	1880–1886§	1881–1887
1974–75		E3/4	1890–1898§	1891–1899
1986–90		E3/5	1900–1980§	1901–1981

§ Even numbers only

The 'East Berlin' numbers are shown below *in italics:*

Class	Motor cars (even)		Trailer cars (odd)	
E3/1	1802–1844	*101.002–101.044*	1803–1845	*151.003–151.045*
E3/2	1850–1876	*102.050–102.076*	1851–1877	*152.051–152.077*
E3/3	1880–1886	*103.080–103.086*	1881–1887	*153.081–153.087*
E3/4	1890–1898	*104.090–104.098*	1891–1899	*154.091–154.099*
E3/5	1900–1980	*105.100–105.080*	1901–1981	*155.101–155.181*

The Present Rolling Stock

All trains now in service on the U-Bahn are of post-war vintage, the oldest dating back to 1956. Notwithstanding that the large profile lines were built after the small profile routes, our survey at the current rolling stock should begin with the former, as the latter's trains were clearly 'smaller' adapted derivatives.

What is known as the 'D' group of stock began with a two-car motor-motor prototype in 1956, with the production series beginning in 1957-58. In all, a total of 432 cars were built between 1956 and 1971 by Orenstein & Koppel (O&K) and Deutsche Waggon-und Maschinenfabrik (DWM), the relevant builds having their sub-classifications of D.56, D.57, D.60, D.63, D.65, DL.65, DL.68 and DL.70, ultimately comprising 230 cars of type D and 202 of type DL, the latter type being constructed of light metal. All cars are numbered in pairs, upwards from 2000-2001 to 2430-2431 and can now be found on lines U5, U6 and U7. With an all-yellow exterior livery (the original waist-line aluminium strip around the body has since been removed), interior seating is wholly longitudinal at 36 per car plus a tip-up seat in the trailing end communicating door. The decor comprises a formica-type panelling with a wood grain effect.

In 1988-89, some 98 vehicles of the 1957-60 type were sold to East Berlin, to operate on line E (today's line U5), needed for the eastern extension from Tierpark to Hönow. The cars were not actually paid for in cash but as a credit, off-set against payment for current used by BVG on lines which passed under East Berlin (U6 and U8) and for the repairs to the tracks and tunnels. The cars were painted in a revised livery – white with yellow passenger doors and front cab ends beneath the roof line 'lip'. Before dispatch the trains were given a thorough overhaul, and other work undertaken included the conversion of the trainstop apparatus and the fitting of optical/acoustic door closing signals. These 98 cars (see list opposite) were numbered to the UIC standard, having seven digits in all. The first three numbers indicated the class, the next three the vehicle number and the last, a 'control' digit, is calculated by a complex formula, to verify the integrity of the main number. Some 48 cars of the D stock used on East Berlin line U5 have been transferred back onto lines U6 and U7 and all of it was subsequently renumbered back into the 2xxx series from July 1992. Some still remain in the white and yellow doors livery, while others have already been painted in the smart BVG all-yellow colour.

Out of the fleet of 432 cars (216 two-car units), two cars (2000-2001) are now used for rail greasing purposes, while 2050-2051 have been withdrawn following damage at Biesdorf-Süd in July 1992.

The various batches of the large profile 'D' stock can now be found in service on lines U5, U6 and U7 and the narrow profile A3 stock is based on that design. A D.63 motor car is at the rear of this six-car train on line U7 at Hermannplatz. Note the 'bridge' over the train – this is where line U8 passes over U7 at this station – all underground.
Brian Hardy

D Stock Summary

Numbers	Type	No.	Built By	Year	East Berlin numbers / Notes
2000–2001	D.56	2	O&K	1956	
2002–2003 to 2018–2019	D.57	18	O&K	1957–58	110.300/301 to 110.316/317
2020–2021	D.57	2	O&K	1957	
2022–2023 to 2026–2027	D.57	6	O&K	1957–58	110.318/319 to 110.322/323
2028–2029 to 2052–2053	D.57	26	DWM	1957–58	110.324/325 to 110.348/349
2054–2055 to 2058–2059	D.60	6	O&K	1960–61	
2060–2061 to 2070–2071	D.60	12	O&K	1960–61	110.350/351 to 110.360/361
2072–2073	D.60	2	O&K	1960–61	
2074–2075	D.60	2	O&K	1960–61	110.364/365
2076–2077	D.60	2	O&K	1960–61	
2078–2079 to 2082–2083	D.60	6	O&K	1960–61	110.368/369 to 110.372/373
2084–2085 to 2098–2099	D.60	16	DWM	1960–61	110.374/375 to 110.388/389
2100–2101	D.60	2	DWM	1960–61	
2102–2103 to 2112–2113	D.60	12	DWM	1960–61	110.390/391 to 110.400/401
2114–2115 to 2148–2149	D.63	36	O&K	1963–64	
2150–2151 to 2184–2185	D.63	36	DWM	1963–64	
2186–2187 to 2228–2229	D.65	44	O&K	1965	
2230–2231 to 2234–2235	DL.65	6	O&K	1965–66	Lightweight cars
2236–2237 to 2302–2303	DL.68	68	O&K	1968–70	Lightweight cars
2304–2305 to 2370–2371	DL.68	68	DWM	1968–70	Lightweight cars
2372–2373 to 2430–2431	DL.70	60	O&K	1970–71	Lightweight cars
Total:		432			

Two-car trains on the large profile lines can be seen on U6, U8 and U9, but only early on Sunday mornings. D.65 two-car set 2195-2194 pauses at Alexanderplatz on line U8 on 26 June 1994, prior to line U8 becoming worked completely by F.90/92 stock. *Jeanne Hardy*

Although the interior of the D stock is similar in appearance to the A3 narrow profile type, its spaciousness is evident here. Some D stock have tilting opening windows on one side of the car only, while others have them on both sides, as seen here. However, in the case of the latter, one side is kept locked closed. *Brian Hardy*

The D.57/60 types that were sent to East Berlin for use on line 'E' were given a new livery – yellow and white – along with several other modifications. D.57 motor coach 2035 leads on line U5 at Grottkauer Strasse in June 1993. *Steve Williams*

The small profile version of the D stock is the A.3 and A3.L types, comprising 344 cars built between 1960 and 1973, also by O&K and DWM and also in motor-motor pairs. Interior layout is similar to their larger counterparts and the outward front-end appearance is similar. However, the difference in size is most noticeable, with one window separating each pair of double doors instead of two as on the large profile stock. It is interesting to note that the narrow profile stock is numbered downwards from 999 and therefore the oldest cars have higher numbers and the newest the lowest. Numbered in pairs from 998-999 to 656-657, the sub-classifications which denote the period of build are A3.60, A3.64, A3.66, A3L.66, A3L.67 and A3L.71, summarised as follows:

Numbers	Type	No.	Built By	Year	Notes
998–999 to 984–985	A3.60	16	DWM	1960–61	
982–983 to 934–935	A3.64	50	O&K	1964	
932–933 to 912–913	A3.66	22	DWM	1966	
910–911 to 892–893	A3.66	20	O&K	1966	
890–891 to 884–885	A3L.66	8	O&K	1966	Lightweight cars
882–883 to 794–795	A3L.67	90	O&K	1967–68	Lightweight cars
792–793 to 656–657	A3L.71	138	O&K	1972–73	Lightweight cars
Total:		344			

The A3 stock in its present form on line U2, leaving Nollendorfplatz on 28 June 1995 and descending the ramp to the tunnels. This was the section of line which closed on 1 January 1972 and re-opened on 13 November 1993. The leading unit is type A3.64. *Brian Hardy*

Narrow profile line U1 at its 'temporary' (for 34 years) terminus, Schlesisches Tor, on 25 May 1986, with a train of type A3L.67. This stock, along with its larger 'D' type counterparts, had waistline beading from new, being later removed to reduce maintenance costs. *John Laker*

The seating capacity of each car is 26 longitudinally, including a tip-up seat on the trailing end communicating door. The last batch of this type, the A3L.71, has a slightly reduced standing capacity (102 instead of 104), caused by the driving cab length being 1,430 mm instead of 1,330 mm and the leading vestibule length being 1,658 mm instead of 1,758 mm.

A total of 16 A3L.71 unit pairs were equipped with Seltrac ATO equipment. These were as follows, with the trains currently allocated to line 4 marked with an asterisk:

682-683*	692-693*	706-707*	718-719*
684-685	696-697	708-709	732-733
688-689*	700-701*	712-713	748-749*
690-691*	702-703*	716-717*	758-759

All other units of this type can be found universally on lines U1, U2 and U15, apart from 998–999, which is used for rail cleaning.

Line U4 operated in ATO mode between 1981 and 1993, for which a small number of A3L.71 trains were specially adapted. Unit 701-700 is at Bayerischer Platz on 29 June 1994 and shows the roof-mounted orange door-open indicator lights and the (lower) red door-close lights. *Brian Hardy*

An all-over-advertisement livery has been applied to narrow profile A3.66 two-car unit 908-909. A two-coach set of F.84 stock (2778-2779) on line U7 has been similarly treated but by a different sponsor. *Capital Transport*

All narrow profile trains have longitudinal seats only. This view shows the interior of A3L.67 motor coach 873. *Brian Hardy*

The modern narrow profile stock is the A3L.82 and A3L.92 type, easily recognisable by its wrap-round cab windows. This is one of the first batch of 1982 origin seen on line U1 at Schlesisches Tor on 25 May 1986. *John Laker*

A3L.92/1 motor car 607 is at the rear of an eight-car train on line U2 at Schönhauser Allee on 29 June 1994. *Brian Hardy*

A3L.92/2 two-car unit 598-599 under test when new in Grunewald depot yard, which is adjacent to Olympia-Stadion (Ost) station on line U2. The last batch of this type of stock, the A3L.92/3, is currently being delivered. *Brian Hardy*

Interior of A3L.92/1 motor coach 620. *Capital Transport*

The wide profile fleet now comprises two types – the aforementioned D type and the 'F' type, introduced from 1973. As with its predecessor, a two-coach prototype motor-motor train was built, numbered 2500-2501. The production series trains continued on over the period 1974-1992, built by O&K and Waggon Union (WU). The complete fleet of type F comprised 514 vehicles, with the numbers ending at 3012-3013. The sub-classes are F.74, F.76, F.79/1, F.79/2, F.84, F.87, F.90 and F.92. This new stock introduced some transverse seating and later batches had a brighter interior, replacing the wood finish look. The exterior design of the prototypes and the first production batch was similar to the D type, but lacked the roof dome 'lip' and stainless steel 'lip' above the windows and doors, giving a smoother finish. The design was altered further in 1976 with 'wrap-round' cab windows were introduced from 2555-2556, while the F.84 and three subsequent batches introduced a black painted section around the cab windows (the 'one-piece' window illusion) and sliding doors were replaced by 'plug' doors. Today the 'F' type can be seen on lines U6 and U7 (sharing its service on both lines with the D type), U8 and U9.

The interior seating capacity of the F.74 and F.76 types is 38, comprising 32 transverse seats and six longitudinal, along with one tip-up seat on the end communicating door and two single tip-up seats by the leading doors. Unit 2606-2607 however, has had one transverse seating bay replaced by three longitudinal seats per side, reducing the main seating capacity from 38 to 36. This set the standard for the F.79 type onwards, although from the F.84 batch, the tip-up seats no longer were provided in the end communicating doors. Paving the way for future rolling stock, unit 2770-2771 has been modified and rebuilt at its trailing ends, to provide complete intercirculation within the two-car unit.

The first group of the 'F' type has a similar appearance to the previous 'D' type, but lacks the roof line front lip, side roof line edge and has a different arrangement of head and tail lights. Fitted with ATO, F74/1 motor car 2507 is seen on line U9. *Capital Transport*

The F.76 stock was the first of the 'F' group to have wrap-round cab windows. Here, 2676 is approaching Seidel-strasse on line U6 and is of type F.79/2, seen on 30 June 1995. *Brian Hardy*

The southern terminus of line U6 is Alt-Mariendorf, where a train of F.79/2 stock disgorges its passengers on 27 June 1994. Note the letters 'SEE' in the cab window, denoting its allocation to Seestrasse depot. *Brian Hardy*

The later 'F' type operates on line U7 (F.84/87/90) and U8 (F.90/92). The exterior appearance changed from earlier batches in having sliding 'plug' doors and a black-painted area around the cab windows, giving the appearance of a one-piece windscreen. An F.90 train pauses at Hermannplatz on line U7, the U-Bahn's longest line, on 28 June 1995. *Brian Hardy*

The various builds are summarised as follows:

Numbers	Type	No.	Built By	Year	Notes
2500–2501	F.74/0	2	O&K	1973	Prototype ATO for line U9
2502–2503 to 2528–2529	F.74/1	28	O&K	1974–75	Equipped with ATO for line U9
2530–2531 to 2548–2549	F.74/2	20	O&K	1974–75	Equipped with ATO for line U9
2550–2551 to 2554–2555	F.74/3	6	O&K	1974–75	Equipped with ATO for line U9
2556–2557 to 2606–2607	F.76	52	O&K	1976–78	Equipped with ATO for line U9 First batch with wrap-round cab windows.
2608–2609 to 2636–2637	F.76	30	WU	1976–78	Equipped with ATO for line U9
2638–2639 to 2656–2657	F.79/1	20	WU	1980–81	Equipped with ATO for line U9
2658–2659 to 2670–2671	F.79/1	14	WU	1980–91	
2672–2673 to 2710–2711	F.79/2	40	O&K	1979–80	
2712–2713 to 2722–2723	F.79/3	12	O&K	1980–81	
2724–2725 to 2800–2801	F.84	78	WU	1984–85	First batch with wrap-round black cab windows and plug doors
2802–2803 to 2842–2843	F.87	42	WU	1986–87	
2844–2845 to 2902–2903	F.90	60	WU	1991–92	
2904–2905 to 3012–3013	F.92	110	WU	1992–94	
Total:		514			

Line U8 is now operated wholly by F.90/92 trains, as seen at Alexanderplatz with a train heading south to Leinestrasse. The southern terminus of U8 will become Hermanstrasse when the new extension opens, providing interchange with the S-Bahn 'Ring' lines S45 and S46. *Brian Hardy*

The 'F' group of stock introduced some transverse seating, the previous 'D' class having all longitudinal seating. Some of the 'F' stock also retains some 'wood' look as seen with this interior of an F.79 motor car on line U6. Note the tip-up seat mounted in the communicating door. *Jeanne Hardy*

In contrast, the F.90/92 stock seen here has a 'grey' wood-grain laminate finish. *Brian Hardy*

The narrow profile lightweight derivative of the F stock was introduced in 1982. It incorporated the wrap-round cab windows of the 1976 large profile trains, but the transverse seating was not perpetuated for restricted space reasons. Numbers began at 654-655 and continue (downwards) to 538-539, comprising types A3L.82 and A3L.92, the latter comprising three batches, the last of which is still being delivered and is to augment services, following the reopening to Warschauer Strasse. This type comprises 116 cars, all of which seat 26 passengers longitudinally, with no tip-up seats. They mostly operate on line U2, but can also be found in small numbers on line U1. The batches were built as follows:

Numbers	Type	No.	Built By	Year
654–655 to 640–641	A3L.82	14	WU	1982–83
638–639 to 604–605	A3L.92/1	36	ABB/WU	1993–94
602–603 to 554–555	A3L.92/2	50	ABB	1994
552–553 to 538–539	A3L.92/3	16	ABB	1995
Total:		116		

A third type of narrow profile rolling stock, which had no bearing on any large profile counterparts, was the G stock, all of which was built by Lokomotivbau Elektrotechnische Werke 'Hans Beimler' for East Berlin line A (the disconnected piece of what is now part of line U2) between Mohrenstrasse and Vinetastrasse. The 242 cars were built in batches between 1975 and 1989 and differed in almost every respect from anything that had gone before. Quite simply, their appearance can be described as a 'box on wheels', being extremely angular. There are no front cab doors and each car has only two pairs of double doors along each side, making boarding and alighting at stations that bit slower. Formed into two-car (motor-non driving motor) pairs, two units minimum are thus required for a train, four being the maximum. The trains were numbered in the 7-figure UIC system, although since reunification they have been renumbered (downwards), even numbers being driving motors, odd numbers non-driving motors, in the series from 498-499 to 266-267.

The 1975 eight-car prototype train was distinguishable by having a narrower driving cab window than on the production vehicles with a separate destination blind above and a different head- and tail-light layout. The side car and door windows were at a slightly higher level and did not follow the lower contour of the front cab window. The production cars have the destination blind incorporated at top left of the wide front cab window, while the car side and door windows follow the lower line of the front cab windows. A total of 114 cars were thus built between 1975 and 1983, and inclusive of the prototype were known as type GI. The UIC numbers were from 135.750/751 to 135.862/863.

A further batch of 24 cars of type GII were built in 1983, but first served on the Piräus – Athens – Kifissia Railway during 1984 and 1985. Motor cars were numbered 101-112 and non-driving motors 201-212. Whilst in service in Athens the cars were fitted with an exterior side 'skirt' at floor level, because of the gap between the train and platform. On their delivery to East Berlin in 1985-87 minus their temporary 'skirts', they became (in sequence) 135.864/865 to 135.887/888 (ex-101/201 to 112/212 respectively) and were operationally compatible with their GI type predecessors.

The G stock was built in batches between 1975 and 1989 for East Berlin line 'A', now the northern section of line U2, and was numbered in the 7-figure scheme. Heading south at Schönhauser Allee on 23 May 1986 is a train bound for Otto-Grotewohl-Strasse, now named Mohrenstrasse. The car nearest the camera is 135.802-2 of type G1 of 1980, and is now numbered 448.
Bob Greenaway

The last batch of G stock comprised 104 vehicles built in 1988/89 to replace the remaining old U-Bahn small profile stock on line A, which was achieved on 5 November 1989. This batch was classified type GI/I and these cars were not able to operate with their older GI and GII counterparts. These cars were numbered 135.896/897 to 135.998/999. Motor cars seat 30 and non driving motors 36, all longitudinally. The summary of G stock is as follows:

Numbers	Type	No.	Year
135.750/751 to 135.756/757	GI	8	1975
135.758/759 to 135.772/773	GI	16	1978
135.774/775 to 135.794/795	GI	22	1979
135.796/797 to 135.836/837	GI	42	1980
135.838/839 to 135.852/853	GI	16	1981
135.854/855 to 135.856/857	GI	4	1982
135.858/859 to 135.862/863	GI	6	1983
135.864/865 to 135.886/887	GII	24	1983
135.896/897 to 135.998/999	GI/I	104	1988–89
Total:		242	

When in May 1991 the Berlin Senate decided to proceed with the re-linking of the two sections of line U2, the question of the inter-availability of trains had to be considered. Whilst the performance characteristics of the G stock were very similar to those of BVG trains, there were several technical differences between the classes and they could not be coupled in multiple. Neither could either of the former western or eastern classes run on the lines of the other system without considerable alteration. As there were fewer of class G, it was decided to rebuild them to western standards.

The G stock now operates on lines U2 and U15, with occasional forays on U1. A mixed livery train with G1/1 motor car 350 leading is seen at Olympia-Stadion (Ost) heading for Ruhleben, despite what is stated on the destination blind. *Brian Hardy*

The interior of the G stock is as austere as its exterior, as seen in this motor coach looking towards the non-driving end. *Brian Hardy*

The main alterations consisted of the reversal of the polarity from minus to plus, to allow class G to collect current from the western third rail, and the replacement of the mechanical roof-mounted trainstops by a magnetic ones. The passenger emergency signal had also to be changed to give a signal only while the train was in motion, and not bring it to an immediate stop. The door-closing mechanism was also linked to the controller, so that a train could not move off until all the doors were closed. The speed-limiting device on the controller also had to be altered to allow the trains to run at 60 km/hr maximum, as permitted on some sections of the western network. A new cab radio had to be installed and finally the destination indicators had to be refitted to show all possible destinations on the narrow profile network. The rebuilding work was carried out during 1992 and 1993 both by the builders of the class in Hennigsdorf and by the Schöneweide workshops of DR. Prior to this, however, the first GI train was transferred from the BVB to BVG on 9 December 1990 (sets 135.896-899), commencing trial runs on the narrow profile network on 17 December. It was not until 4 November 1992 that the first GI train ran in service on the then line U1 between Ruhleben and Schlesisches Tor (sets 306/7, 308/9, 342/3 and 348/9). When the through service was institued on 13 November 1993, G stock worked regularly alongside all of the varying types of the A3 stock, built from 1960 to date. However, it was found that, as the class had fewer doors per car, G stock had longer dwell times in stations with, over a period, a harmful effect of service regularity. Some of these sets have therefore been transferred away from U2 and can be found on the perhaps less demanding U15.

Like other trains hitherto solely in service in East Berlin, most of the G class was renumbered into the simpler three-figure (or four-figure on other stock) system. However, because of withdrawals and premature scrapping due to accidents, eight cars out of the 242 were not renumbered. These were 135.834/835 and 135.868/869 (scrapped after an accident at Spittelmarkt in March 1990), along with 135.780/781 and 135.864/865, which were stored withdrawn. The renumbering can be summarised thus – all groups in ascending or descending respective sequence as applicable:

No.	Previous Number	Year Built	No.
266–267 to 368–369	135.998/999 to 135.896/897	1988–89	104
370–371 to 386–387	135.886/887 to 135.870/871	1983 (Athens 112/212 to 104/204)	18
388–389	135.866/867	1983 (Athens 102–202)	2
390–391 to 416–417	135.862/863 to 135.836/837	1980–83	28
418–419 to 468–469	135.832/833 to 135.782/783	1979–80	52
470–471 to 490–491	135.778/779 to 135.758/759	1978–79	22
492–493 to 498–499	135.756/757 to 135.750/751	1975	8
			234

The last batch of G stock was built in 1988-89 and is still complete, although many of the earlier examples have been withdrawn. Motor car 306 heads a four-car train westwards at Kottbusser Tor, bound for Uhlandstrasse, in September 1995. *Capital Transport*

Following reunification, the large amount of spare stock that hitherto existed was deemed unnecessary and some of the earlier examples of G stock (1975-83) have recently been withdrawn. The withdrawn cars comprise 30 two-car sets (inclusive of 14 of the cars that first served in Athens), the eight withdrawn 1975 prototype cars and the non-renumbered cars (i.e. those still bearing the 'East' seven-figure numbering system).

Prior to August 1994, the interchangeability of stocks between lines meant that no train (either U-Bahn or S-Bahn) carried a 'line' route diagram. A train on line U7 on one day, for example, may be in service on line U8 the next and therefore they all had a combined U- and S-Bahn system diagram. Since August 1994, however, all U-Bahn cars show a 'LINE' diagram, as trains are now normally used on the same line each day – although it is still possible to change cars between lines. On the narrow profile lines, a combined line diagram of U1, U2 and U15 is shown (with U4 on a separate diagram), while on the large profile trains, each line has a separate line diagram.

The BVG has experimented with automatic train operation (ATO) over a number of years on both narrow and large profile lines. Following trials in the Gleisdreieck area on the closed section of line U2, the first in passenger service was on line U9 with Siemens equipment from 13 December 1977, over the whole route, but one train only. Some 28 units were subsequently equipped, followed by a further 41, completing the complete U9 fleet. ATO on U9 is rarely used now, but if it is, it is usually at weekends. A 'Seltrac' system of ATO was introduced on the short line U4 from 4 May 1981, which was funded by the Bundesministerium für Forschung und Technologie – the Federal Ministry for Research and Technology. The trains equipped for ATO also had the lever-operated sliding door handles replaced by push buttons (as found on the London Docklands B.90/92 stock). The Seltrac ATO equipment was removed on 29 November 1993. Of course, all of the U-Bahn is one-person-operated, anyway.

For the large profile lines, a completely new generation of trains has been planned, starting with two six-coach prototypes. Known as type 'HG', on 29 September 1995 the roll-out took place at the Reinickendorf (Berlin) factory of ABB-Henschel of the first of 115 trains. This is the first U-Bahn train in Germany to consist of several (six) close-coupled cars, with passenger intercirculation. While the main part of the work was carried out at ABB-Henschel itself, AEG Rail Vehicles were responsible for the electrical apparatus.

The bodywork is of aluminium and is of integral construction. For the first time, all electrical wiring and apparatus is kept clear of the passenger area, allowing maximum space, and has instead been placed in the driving cab, under the roof or on the underside. All the internal fittings, such as seats, partitions, grab poles and the covering of the inside walls, allow complete freedom in the arrangement of the passenger saloons and can, if desired, be removed and replaced without extensive alterations to the body. As the longitudinal seats are fastened to the bodyside walls, cleaning is easy.

A train of HG stock, which began delivery in 1995. *AEG*

The six cars of the train are connected by corridor gangways. These are panelled internally and can scarcely be distinguished from outside. They allow an almost unimpeded view throughout the entire train. By a combination of attractive design and adoption of anti-graffiti material, it is hoped to reduce the potential for vandalism. The interior is panelled in fire-resistant, tear-resistant material, which can be recycled and presents a clear and uncluttered welcoming appearance.

The 18 doors on each side of the six-car train allow a clear opening, of 1,300mm, to give convenient boarding and alighting. A light signal on the body side tells visually-impaired passengers the location of the doors. While the train is in service, the floor level is constantly monitored to guarantee a step-free entry at stations.

The clear and spacious driving cabs have, with 78% glazing, the greatest such area of any underground trains in service anywhere in the world. On the window, which is made of toughened safety glass, a black mask covers the lower part. Headlights and tail lights are incorporated in one unit. Behind the driving position, a window allows a clear view of the passenger saloon.

A new three-step control system not only minimises collision damage at shunting speeds but also limits any damage to the cars by movement in service. This system works through rubber and viscose-elastic elements in the coupling between the cars. The secondary suspension, of the bodies, is air-based.

A new heating and ventilation system has been developed for the class 'H'. Air is drawn in through the roof and distributed into the passenger space through ventilation channels in the ceiling. The air is changed 50 times per hour. For heating, the fresh air is mixed with the air from the saloon and distributed by channels under the seating. The driving cab is separately heated and ventilated. There is an IBIS system for passenger information with a public address system, and visual displays at the connections between the cars.

The train is powered by 24 three-phase asynchronous motors of 90kW each, to give a total power output of 2,160kW. There are two motors in each bogie, these bogies being of a new type developed by ABB-Henschel to reduce the unsprung weight. Each group of eight motors is separately cooled and the chopper is fitted with GTO to allow a smooth transition from acceleration to braking. Two computers allow supervision of all on-board apparatus and the diagnosis of faults. The driving position is fitted with a colour display to give continuous information on the entire train and workshop personnel can also use this as an interface for the diagnosis of faults, thereby lessening the time not in service. There is also a 110V d.c. on-board system for the control system, ventilation and lighting, but the heating is fed directly from the main current supply. Six of the twelve bogies carry current pick up on each side.

The trains have been designed for future conversion to (completely) automatic train operation, in which case the driving positions will be removed and the passenger saloons extended to the outer car ends.

It is expected that the first two trains, which are prototypes, will undergo thorough testing starting from February 1996 before series delivery of the 46 trains from the first order begins in 1997. The entire delivery, including the option for 69 additional trains, is worth DEM 1.4-milliard.

For the future, 25 four-car trains of type 'HK' are to be built by ABB Henschel for the narrow profile system and delivery is expected from the end of 1996.

At the presentation of the type 'HG', a mock-up of the narrow profile type 'HK', now under development, was shown. This will be a four-car unit of 51,640mm length, the width being the usual 2,300mm. Like type 'HK', the narrow profile version will have end-to-end access. It is expected that delivery of the first of 25 trains on order will begin in 1997 with the balance being delivered by the end of 1999.

The principal technical details of the new 'HG' train are as follows:

Length over coupling:	98,740mm
Leading/rear car length:	15,800mm
Intermediate car length:	15,650mm
Car width:	2,650mm
Bogie spacing:	9,500mm
Wheelbase:	1,800mm
Wheel diameter:	700mm
Floor level above track:	950mm
Unladen weight:	138.5 tonnes
Maximum passenger capacity:	724
Seating (including folding seats):	208
Standing capacity at 4 persons/m^2	516
Maximum acceleration (m/s^2)	1.3
Maximum speed (km/hr):	70

Current Stock Statistics
All measurements are in millimetres.

Type	No. series	Body length over coupler	Height roof to rail top	Width	Seats:		
					Longitudinal	Transverse	Tip-up
A3.60 to A3L.71	999-656	12,830	3,180	2,300	26	-	1
A3L.82 to A3L.92	655-538	12,910	3,180	2,300	26	-	-
G (Motor)	489-266	12,830	3,190	2,360	30	-	-
G (NDM)		12,830	3,190	2,360	36	-	-
D/DL	2000-2431	15,850	3,425	2,650	36	-	1
F.74	2500-2555	16,050	3,432	2,650	6	32	3
F.76	2556-2605	16,050	3,432	2,650	6	32	3
F.76	2606-2607	16,050	3,432	2,650	12	24	3
F.76	2608-2637	16,050	3,425	2,650	6	32	3
F.79	2638-2723	16,050	3,425	2,650	12	24	3
F.84/87	2724-2843	16,050	3,425	2,640	12	24	2
F.90/92	2844-3013	16,050	3,419	2,640	12	24	2

Rolling Stock Summary – Small Profile

A3 Stock				G Stock		
M		M		M	NDM	
16	A3.60	16	A3L.82	26	26	GI (1978–83)
50	A3.64	36	A3L.92/1	5	5	GII (1983 Athens)
20	A3.66 (O&K)	50	A3L.92/2	52	52	GI/I (1988–89)
22	A3.66 (DWM)	16	A3L.92/3			
8	A3.66			83	83	
90	A3.67					
138	A3L.71					
		462	Total vehicles		166	Total vehicles

The figures for the A3 stock of 462 vehicles will enable 57 eight-car trains to be formed (43x8 A3.60 to A3L.71 and 14x8 A3L.82 to A3L.92) with three spare two-car sets. The G stock enables 20 eight-car trains to be formed (13 type GI/I and 7 type GI & GII), with three spare two-car sets of types GI & GII.

Rolling Stock Summary – Large Profile

D Stock		F Stock	
M		M	
2	D.56	2	F.74 (Prototype ATO)
26	D.57 (O&K)	54	F.74 (ATO)
24	D.57 (DWM)	52	F.76 (ATO – O&K)
30	D.60 (O&K)	30	F.76 (ATO – WU)
30	D.60 (DWM)	8	F.79/1 (ATO)
36	D.63 (O&K)	26	F.79/1
36	D.63 (DWM)	40	F.79/2
44	D.65	12	F.79/3
6	DL.65	78	F.84
136	DL.68	42	F.87
60	DL.70	60	F.90
		110	F.92
430	Total Vehicles	514	Total Vehicles

The above figures comprise 215 units of D stock and 257 units of F stock, making a total of 472 units or 944 cars.

	Trains for service	Composition	Units	Line Units	Cars
Line 5	29	29x6	87	96	192
Line 6*	31	31x4	62	79	158
Line 7*	39	39x6	117	158	316
Line 8	18	18x6	54	66	132
Line 9	19	19x6	57	73	146
Totals	136	31x4 105x6	377	472	944

Note: * Line 6 47xD and 32xF, line 7 72xD and 86xF.

U-Bahn Stations

Like Paris, but unlike London, most of the Berlin U-Bahn is underground. Only the sections quoted below are in the open air, either at ground level, in a cutting, or elevated on viaduct and it will be seen that the later lines (U7 to U9) are wholly underground:

Line	Stations/Section	No. of Stations
U1	Podbielskiallee - Krumme Lanke	6
U2	Ruhleben - Olympia-Stadion (Ost)	2
U2	Nollendorfplatz - Gleisdreieck	3
U2	Eberswalder Strasse - Schönhauser Allee	2
U4	Rathaus Schöneberg (in 'tunnel' but 'open' at sides)	1
U5	Biesdorf-Süd - Wuhletal	3
U5	Kaulsdorf-Nord - Hönow	6
U6	Scharnweberstrasse - Holzhauser Strasse	3

A feature of many U-Bahn stations is that they are of the island platform type – in fact the great majority, as will be seen in the table below. There are, of course, a number with side platforms, and some others offer cross-platform interchange (e.g. at Wittenbergplatz on U1/2 and Mehringdamm on U6/7) while some have two pairs of platforms (e.g. Deutsche Oper on U2).

Much of the original section of the Berlin U-Bahn was in the open and on viaduct. Hallesches Tor, on lines U1 and U15, perches above and beside the Landwehrkanal. Line U6 also serves Hallesches Tor, but underground. *John Laker*

Station Type Summary

Station Type	U1	U15	U2	U4	U5	U6	U7	U8	U9	Total
Tunnel	10	5*	20	5	11	26	40	23	18	158
Open-air	14	8*	7	-	9	3	-	-	-	41
Total	**24**	**13***	**27**	**5**	**20**	**29**	**40**	**23**	**18**	**199**

Interchange	U1	U15	U2	U4	U5	U6	U7	U8	U9	Total
U-Bahn	8	7*	5	2	-	4	7	3	5	41
S-Bahn	2	1	3	1	3	2	3	4	2	21
U- & S-Bahn	-	-	2	-	1	-	-	1	1	5
None	14	5*	17	2	16	23	30	15	10	132
Total	**24**	**13***	**27**	**5**	**20**	**29**	**40**	**23**	**18**	**199**

Platform Type	U1	U15	U2	U4	U5	U6	U7	U8	U9	Total
Island	14	4*	16	4	16	26	36	22	15	153
Side	7	6*	8	-	-	1	1	1	1	25
Other	3	3*	3	1	4	2	3	-	2	21
Total	**24**	**13***	**27**	**5**	**20**	**29**	**40**	**23**	**18**	**199**

* Line U15 stations shared with line U1 and actual stations solely on U15 comprise Uhlandstrasse, Kurfürstendamm and Wittenbergplatz.

The terminus of lines U1 and U15 was Schlesisches Tor after the Wall went up on 13 August 1961. The station has been restored to its original German Renaissance style. *Steve Williams*

In architectural terms, the Berlin U-Bahn is much less well-known than either the Paris or Moscow Métro, or the London Underground. This may in some measure be due to the considerable losses sustained during the bombardments of 1944-45. Nevertheless, the U-Bahn buildings did, and in many cases, still do, have merit and deserve closer study.

The first Director of the Hochbahngesellschaft, Paul Wittig, was also an architect and had been project leader for the building of the Reichstag until 1894. He himself designed certain stations, such as Prinzenstrasse and also other structures, for example the viaduct over the Landwehrkanal and the original power station at Trebbiner Strasse. However, perhaps his greatest contribution to the architecture of the system was his invitation in 1900 to Professor Alfred Grenander (1863-1931) to work with him on the project. Grenander was responsible for many of the stations on the first lines and today is remembered principally for the reconstructed station building of Wittenbergplatz (1913). He also designed the trains of classes A1 and A2, but his responsibilities did not end there, since he was involved also in detail matters, such as ticket offices and the design of the pillars supporting the viaducts on elevated stretches. While much of this has gone over the years, either in war damage or rebuilding, much continues to survive and can be seen in locations such as Bülowstrasse. In general, the work was executed with rich detail in the wealthier western districts, while the eastern areas had to be content with much plainer designs. The building and stations on the line to Nordring were much simpler.

Wittenbergplatz was built at the turn of the century but was rebuilt in Art Nouveau style in 1913 and all its best traditions have been kept in restoration, inside and out. This is the exterior on 24 June 1993. *Steve Williams*

The ticket hall area of Wittenbergplatz as seen on 23 May 1986. *Alan Blake*

In 1952, at the 50th anniversary of the U-Bahn in Berlin, London Transport presented the BVG with an early post-war (i.e. unlined) station name bullseye, which can be seen proudly on display at Wittenbergplatz on the westbound platform of line U2. *Capital Transport*

Grenander was clearly an unusually gifted architect and one who did not confine his work to one style. Having produced work with the abundant detail of the Wilhelmine period, he then, after 1918, was able to change completely and design buildings in an advanced modern style, which was in many ways an inspiration for London Transport. Buildings from his second period include those at Krumme Lanke and Olympia-Stadion.

Of course, many other architects worked on projects for the U-Bahn over the same period and Schöneberg, ever individual, chose for its architect Johann Emil Schaudt, who made a particular feature of the station entrances.

In the early post-war period, shortage of materials meant that simplicity had to rule and many of the stations on the extensions of the 1950s and early-1960s are plain to the point of dullness. But once sufficient funds were again available, the BVG were able to call upon the talents of a wide range of architects for the designing and fitting of their new stations. Many had been involved but perhaps the greatest contribution has been made by Rainer Rümmler, who designed many stations in the 1970s and 1980s – Johannisthaller Chaussee is an example of his plainer work, Rathaus Steglitz of his more exuberant – and also other features such as the intriguing entrance at Haselhorst.

Designed in 1929 by Alfred Granander in 'new realism' style, this, at Krumme Lanke on U1 and a number of other U- and S-Bahn stations of the time, were similar in design to some of those built for London Underground stations in the 1930s. *Capital Transport*

To be found throughout the U-Bahn and S-Bahn system are these automatic ticket machines – this at Krumme Lanke on line U1. *Capital Transport*

The following will serve as a first-time introductory selection for any visitor to the Berlin U-Bahn:

Line	Station	Notes
U1	Krumme Lanke	One of a number of stations on the Berlin U-Bahn and S-Bahn system which are akin to styles subsequently adopted by London Transport in the 1930's 'Charles Holden' era.
U1	Onkel Toms Hütte	Station is integrated in a local shopping centre with shops on both sides of the tracks.
U1	Dahlem-Dorf	Thatched roof street-level station building.
U1	Heidelberger Platz	'Moscow' type high roof station tunnel with ornate circular exterior entrance building.
U2	Olympia-Stadion (Ost)	Three tracks, four platform faces, much like White City LUL station in layout.
U2	Sophie-Charlotte-Platz	U-Bahn murals on platforms walls in both directions.
U1 U2 U15	Wittenbergplatz	Two island platforms and one single platform (for U15 shuttle), all visible under the same roof. The westbound platform on U2 has an LT 'bullseye' station name sign. The ticket hall has much use of 'wood' and exterior has pleasing concrete finish, restored in 1984 to its 1913 style.
U1/2	Gleisdreieck	Open elevated station with island platforms for each line, U1 above U2 at roughly right angles to each other. On U1 platforms, trains on U2 can be seen arriving and departing at the lower level platforms, and can be seen crossing the river bridge opposite. The disused viaduct of the former S-Bahn are clearly visible from the open-air section of the platforms on line U1.
U2	Klosterstrasse	Island platform station with trackside walls having ceramic murals of examples of past Berlin transport. The northern end of the island platform has the driving cab and section of passenger car of an original Schöneberg U-Bahn train inset in the wall. At the southern end of the station, the old signal lever frame from Alexanderplatz (line U2) can be seen behind glass. The station was restored in 1987.
U2	Märkisches Museum	Scenes and maps of old Berlin can be seen on the walls.
U5	Biesdorf-Süd	Half the service from Alexanderplatz reverses here Mondays to Fridays midday, trains continuing into sidings beyond the station.
U5	Wuhletal	Two island platforms, the inner faces being for U5, the outer faces for S-Bahn line S5, giving cross-platform interchange in both directions.
U6	Kochstrasse	Old style entrance to station, and nearby to the former vehicle border crossing – 'Checkpoint Charlie'.
U7 U8	Hermannplatz	This elegant two-level underground station has been restored to near original condition. Line 7 passes under line 8, the latter being on a 'bridge'.
U7	Rathaus Spandau to Paulsternstrasse	All stations (opened in 1984) with opulent but differing decor schemes.
U8	Franz-Neumann-Platz to Wittenau	Stations opened 1987-94 and built with differing but opulent decor schemes, similar to line U7 (above).

The present Olympia-Stadion (Ost) station was built in 1929–30 in 'New Realism' style, being designed by Professor Alfred Grenander. Its grandiose scale was necessary to cope with crowds to and from the nearby stadium. *Steve Williams*

The platforms of Sophie-Charlotte-Platz on line U2 with murals depicting different U-Bahn themes. *Nick Agnew*

The station building at Dahlem-Dorf on line U1 was designed by Fredrich and Wilhelm Hennings in 1912/13 in "arts and crafts" style, complete with thatched roof. Note the large number of bicycles parked outside the station. *Nick Agnew*

Some of the platform fittings at Dahlem-Dorf are in polished wood; in this case the seats represent people embracing. *Nick Agnew*

Heidelberger Platz was built on a grand and ornate scale both inside and out. The platform level shows its vast vault – an inspiration to the Moscow metro system, perhaps. *Capital Transport*

The street-level entrance to Heidelberger Platz is equally as ornate as at platform level and at the entrance, set in concrete, is the U-Bahn's 'U' symbol. *Alan Blake*

The entrance to Klosterstrasse on line U2, seen in July 1995. The station was renovated and restored in 1986/87.
Brian Hardy

The present wide island platform at Klosterstrasse is because a branch extension of the line was proposed and Klosterstrasse would have had a centre platform. *Jeanne Hardy*

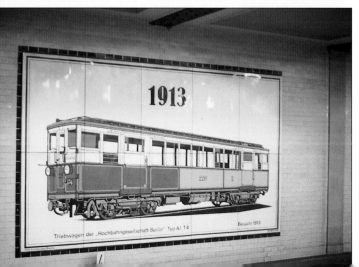

Along the walls opposite the platforms at Klosterstrasse are murals depicting the various types of Berlin public transport in earlier years. This view shows an A1 type motor coach of 1913.
Steve Williams

The Schöneberg U-Bahn line (the present line U4) serves well-to-do areas of Berlin and fittingly, the stations were built to match. The entrance to Viktoria-Luise-Platz is depicted here.
Brian Patton

Stadtpark station was the last U-Bahn station to reopen after the Second World War, on 15 May 1951, but from that date was renamed Rathaus Schöneberg. This station is unique in being 'underground' but open at the sides with windows, complete with venetian blinds!
Nick Agnew

Oskar-Helene-Heim on the 1929 extension of what is now line U1 was designed in 'cottage' style by Friedrich Hennings.
Steve Williams

The extensively decorated stations applied from the 1970s in West Berlin are evident here at Rathaus Steglitz on line U9 (opened 1974), Konstanzer Strasse on U7 (1978) and the entrance to Zitadelle also on U7 (1984).
Nick Agnew (2)
Brian Hardy

Examples of the opulence of the stations on the extensions of line U8 are seen here. Lindauer Allee, which is the only station on U8 which has 'side' platforms, opened in 1994. Franz-Neumann-Platz opened in 1987.
Capital Transport

Left and opposite Four examples of the differing styles on the line U7 extension westwards towards Spandau.
Capital Transport

Rohrdamm

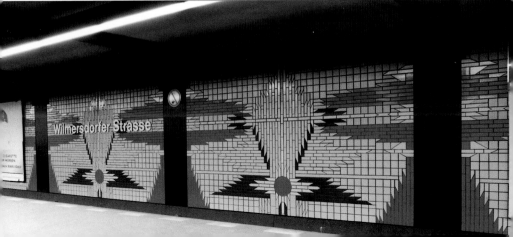

Station Renamings

Stations renamed on the Berlin U-Bahn system are many and varied, most often for 'political' reasons. Those that could be ascertained are listed as follows:

Present lines	Opened	Name	Date Renamed	Renamed
U1/15	18.02.02	Oranienstrasse	14.02.26	**Görlitzer Bahnhof** (Oranienstrasse) Suffix dropped 1982
	18.02.02	Stralauer Tor	15.09.24	Osthafen (Stralauer Tor)
U1/15	17.08.02	Warschauer Brücke	14.10.95	**Warschauer Strasse**
U2	08.06.13	Stadion	01.03.35	Reichssportsfeld
			25.06.50	Olympia-Stadion
			31.05.92	**Olympia-Stadion (Ost)**
U2	29.03.08	Reichskanzlerplatz	24.04.33	Adolf-Hitler-Platz
			17.05.45	Reichskanzlerplatz
			18.12.63	**Theodor-Heuss-Platz**
U2	29.03.08	Kaiserdamm	1936	Kaiserdamm (Messedamm)
			27.04.67	Adenauerdamm (Messedamm)
			15.01.68	**Kaiserdamm (Messedamm)**
U2	14.05.06	Bismarckstrasse	01.08.29	Städtische Oper (Bismarckstrasse)
			16.08.34	Deutsches Opernhaus (Bismarckstrasse)
			22.09.61	Deutsche Oper (Bismarckstrasse)
			28.04.78	**Deutsche Oper**
U2	14.12.02	Knie	02.10.53	**Ernst-Reuter-Platz**
U2	28.09.07	Leipziger Platz	30.01.23	**Potsdamer Platz**
U2	01.10.08	Kaiserhof	18.08.50	Thälmannplatz
			15.04.86	Otto-Grotewohl-Strasse
			03.10.91	**Mohrenstrasse**
U2	01.10.08	Friedrichstrasse	30.01.23	Leipziger Strasse
			15.09.24	Friedrichstadt (Mohrenstrasse)
			01.02.36	**Stadtmitte** (Mohrenstrasse) Suffix dropped 1970
U2	01.07.13	Inselbrücke	01.06.35	**Märkisches Museum**
U2	27.07.13	Schönhauser Tor	01.05.34	Horst-Wessel-Platz
			26.05.45	Schönhauser Tor
			1950	Luxemburgplatz
			01.05.78	**Rosa-Luxemburg-Platz**
U2	27.07.13	Danziger Strasse	Jan–50	Dimitroffstrasse
			03.10.91	**Eberswalder Strasse**
U2	27.07.13	Nordring	01.02.36	**Schönhauser Allee**
U2	29.06.30	Pankow (Vinetastrasse)	13.11.93	**Vinetastrasse**
U4	01.12.10	Stadtpark	15.05.51	**Rathaus Schöneberg**
U4	01.12.10	Hauptstrasse	01.07.33	**Innsbrucker Platz (Hauptstrasse)**
U15	12.10.13	Uhlandstrasse	07.03.49	Uhlandstrasse (Kurfürstendamm)
			02.09.61	**Uhlandstrasse**
U5	21.12.30	Memler Strasse	22.03.50	Marchlewskistrasse
			03.10.91	**Weberwiese**
U5	21.12.30	Petersburger Strasse	03.06.46	Bersarinstrasse
			01.01.58	Bersarinstrasse (Frankfurter Tor)
			Jun–58	Frankfurter Tor
			03.10.91	**Rathaus Friedrichshain**

Present lines	Opened	Name	Date Renamed	Renamed
U5	21.12.30	Frankfurter Allee	1937	Frankfurter Allee (Ringbahn)
			21.12.51	Stalinallee (Ringbahn)
			14.11.61	**Frankfurter Allee (Ringbahn)**
U5	21.12.30	Lichtenberg (Zentralfriedhof)	1935	Bahnhof Lichtenberg (Zentralfriedhof)
			1965	Bahnhof Lichtenberg
			1974	**Lichtenberg**
U5	21.12.30	Friedrichsfelde	01.01.58	**Friedrichsfelde** (Tierpark) Suffix dropped 1970
U5	01.07.89	Albert-Norden-Strasse	03.10.91	**Kaulsdorf-Nord**
U5	01.07.89	Heinz-Hoffmann-Strasse	03.10.91	**Grottkauer Strasse**
U5	01.07.89	Paul-Verner-Strasse	03.10.91	**Louis-Lewin-Strasse**
U6	31.05.58	Tegel	31.05.92	**Alt-Tegel**
U6	31.05.58	Seidelstrasse (Flughafen Tegel)	Nov–74	**Seidelstrasse**
U6	08.03.23	Bahnhof Wedding	1972	**Wedding**
U6	08.03.23	Schwartzkopffstrasse	09.04.51	Walter-Ulbricht-Stadion
			15.03.73	Stadion der Weltjugend
			03.10.91	**Schwartzkopffstrasse**
U6	30.01.23	Stettiner Bahnhof	10.01.51	Nordbahnhof
			03.10.91	**Zinnowitzer Strasse**
U6	30.01.23	Bahnhof Friedrichstrasse	15.09.24	Stadtbahn (Friedrichstrasse)
			01.02.36	Bahnhof Friedrichstrasse
			Feb–76	**Friedrichstrasse**
U6	30.01.23	Kochstrasse	20.10.95	**Kochstrasse (Checkpoint Charlie)**
U2/U6	30.01.23	Leipziger Strasse	15.09.24	Friedrichstadt (Leipziger Strasse)
			01.02.36	Stadtmitte (Leipziger Strasse)
			05.10.92	**Stadtmitte**
U6/U7	19.04.24	Belle-Alliance-Strasse	27.02.46	Franz-Mehring-Strasse
			09.10.47	**Mehringdamm**
U6	14.02.26	Kreuzberg	01.10.37	Flughafen
			01.09.75	**Platz der Luftbrücke**
U6	10.09.27	Flughafen	01.10.37	**Paradestrasse**
U6	22.12.29	Tempelhof (Südring)	1962	Tempelhof Suffix dropped due to the boycott of S-Bahn system
			31.05.92	**Tempelhof (Südring)**
U7	14.12.24	Hesenheide	03.06.33	Kaiser-Friedrich-Platz
			01.01.39	Gardepionierplatz
			09.10.47	**Südstern**
U7	11.04.26	Bergstrasse	04.06.46	Karl-Marx-Strasse
			1962	Neukölln
			31.05.92	**Neukölln (Südring)**
U7	02.01.70	Johannisthaler Chaussee	16.09.72	**Johannisthaler Chaussee (Gropiusstadt)**
U8	06.04.28	Neanderstrasse	31.08.60	**Heinrich-Heine-Strasse**
U8	17.07.27	Schönleinstrasse	02.07.51	Kottbusser Damm (Schönleinstrasse)
			31.05.92	**Schönleinstrasse**
U9	28.08.61	Putlitzstrasse (Westhafen)	31.05.92	**Westhafen**

U-Bahn Power Supply, Signalling and Control

Power Supply

The U-Bahn is operated with direct current at 750V. The first power station was at Trebbiner Strasse near Gleisdreieck, right in the heart of the original network. With the extension of the network, another power station was built near the Unterspree in Spandau (Ruhleben), providing current at 10,000V and a frequency of 40Hz, delivered by substations to the U-Bahn at Deutsches Opernhaus and Senefelderplatz. The U-Bahn of Schöneberg, Wilmersdorf and Dahlem took their current directly from the power station Südwest.

For the new Nordsüdbahn, now part of line U6, substations were built at Wedding and Hallesches Tor, current being delivered from the local electricity power organisation called BEWAG, and stepped down to line voltage. The BEWAG also supplied power for the lines Gesundbrunnen-Neukölln (now parts of lines U7 and U8) and Alexanderplatz-Friedrichsfelde (now part of U5).

Today, current is supplied only from the BEWAG and transformed for the BVG in BVG-owned rectifiers. The BVG has a central control room at Turmstrasse, which supervises all substations in the former West Berlin area. A similar control room for the ex-BVB lines is situated at Alexanderplatz.

Substations are situated about 2-4 kilometres apart along the various lines. Normally, a substation provides two sections with current but at the crossing of two lines it may provide four sections with current. These sections (Bahnspeisebezirke) can be provided with current by two substations. The polarity of the current rail on large profile is negative and the live rail is covered so that current is taken by the collector shoe from underneath. On the small profile network, the polarity of the current rail is positive and the current rail is not covered – current is thus picked up by the collector shoe from above.

For the power supply to its stations, the BVG has its own 6kV cable network which receives current by rectifiers via short circuit limitation facilities or via transformers with two coils. The transformers on the station have an alternating current transformer for light and power and for the supply of the train security/safety equipment. For the escalators there is a separate transformer inside the transformer station. If there is a failure of the transformer station power supply (with the exception of the escalators), there is a connection to a low tension house supply of the public supply network via an isolation transformer.

Signalling

The original signalling on the U-Bahn consisted of mechanical semaphores on the elevated lines and colour light signals on the underground sections. In 1913 automatic block signals were introduced on the section between Spittelmarkt and Nordring *(Schönhauser Allee)*. In 1928 the programme to equip all lines with colour light signals and mechanical trainstops was completed.

All lines are divided into track sections (Blockabschnitte), guarded by a main signal (Blocksignal). Each main signal is combined with a magnetic tripcock (magnetische Fahrsperre). If a train should pass a red signal, the emergency brakes will be applied immediately. The green aspect on a signal is shown only when it is certain that the next signal is clear of trains and that the next main signal is protecting the previous train. Information about line occupancy is provided by track circuits (Gleisstromkreise), operated by short-circuiting ac current passing through the running rails by the wheels and axles of the trains. Other methods, such as tone-frequency circuits, are in use, while in depots electronic axle-counting equipment (elektronische Achszähleinrichtungen) is standard. Stations which have points are provided with signal boxes, the automatic block system being used only between these areas.

The main part of every line is controlled by an area signal box (Regionalstellwerk), the first of which was brought into operation at Tempelhof on 4 January 1971. This controlled the stations of Tempelhof and Platz der Luftbrücke. The second was commissioned between 1971 and 1973, covering the stations Kurfürstenstrasse, Nollendorfplatz, Wittenbergplatz, Kurfürstendamm (upper level) and the other stations on line U4, in the case of Bayerischer Platz the upper level only. During the following years, area signal boxes were brought into service at Seestrasse (with depot), Fehrbelliner Platz (upper level), Deutsche Oper, Krumme Lanke, Hermannplatz and Olympia-Stadion (Ost). Line extensions saw further boxes commissioned at Osloer Strasse (upper and lower levels), Jungfernheide and Rathaus Spandau. All the old electromechanical lever signal boxes were taken out of service while the newer push-button relay boxes of the 1950s and 1960s (Drucktastenrelaisstellwerke) are now operated from the area boxes. The last of the old boxes was decommissioned when the new area box at Prinzenstrasse was opened in 1986. Line U9 is operated by a central box situated at Berliner Strasse (lower level).

The former BVB lines have modern signal boxes, although technically and structurally they differ from those used on lines on what was West Berlin and standardisation will be a problem in the coming years.

The boxes at Tegel, Kurt-Schumacher-Platz, Alt-Mariendorf and Britz-Süd are not controlled by area boxes and will have to be brought into line with this system in the next few years. The newest of these local boxes is that at Uhlandstrasse, brought into operation in March 1983.

In theory, should traffic demand it and stock be available to operate it, it would now be possible to operate a 90-second frequency service on every line.

Train Control

There is no central control for the U-Bahn system as such, but monitoring of all lines is carried out from the Betriebsleitstelle U-Bahn (or BLU) – the service supervision team, which is situated in the BVG headquarters building near Kleistpark on line U7.

Every train driver taking up duty must inform the signal box that he/she is ready to take over a train from another driver, or to bring a train into or out of service. There is a small pool of reserve drivers but in the event of heavy absence, cancellations in the service have to be made. All problems can be relayed to the BLU by radio, for which there are two channels, Ulrich 1 for the small profile lines and Ulrich 2 for the large profile lines. Therefore, train control is almost entirely a matter for the signal box staff.

U-Bahn Train Services, Depots and Operations

The Berlin U-Bahn service offers several interesting comparisons with both the London Underground and the Paris Métro.

In Berlin, services wind down between 00.30 and 01.00 but some 30-40 minutes later on Friday/Saturday and Saturday/Sunday nights. This compares with finishes around 00.30 to 01.00 in London (up to, but not always, an hour earlier on Sundays) and 01.15 in Paris every night. Moreover in recent years (from 6 April 1990), an all-night service has been provided on two Berlin U-Bahn lines on Friday/Saturday and Saturday/Sunday even though Berlin has an excellent all-night bus and tram network. The two weekend night lines are U12 (a combination of U1 between Warschauer Strasse and Wittenbergplatz and U2 between Wittenbergplatz and Ruhleben) and U9, each operating every 15 minutes and providing connections with each other in all directions by having 'stand time' at Zoologischer Garten. Line U12 operates seven trains and line U9 four trains – all four cars.

With most U-Bahn trains formed of motor-motor pairs, uncoupling of trains is simple and is practised on all lines in some form, except for short line U4. The shortest formations are just two cars (normally only seen early on Sunday mornings before 09.00 on U6, U8 and U9), although two-car trains operate daily on U4, and on U15 when operating as a shuttle between Wittenbergplatz and Uhlandstrasse. Maximum train lengths in the peak are eight cars (U2), six cars (U1, U5, U7, U8 and U9), four cars (U15 and U6 – the short length of the 'East Berlin' stations on U6 preclude longer trains at present) and two cars (U4). Most lines reduce to four cars in the evenings, variously between 20.00 and 23.00, but on line U2, the evening formations reduce from eight to six-cars.

It should be noted that Berliners are early risers – the morning peak is between 06.00 and 08.30, the evening peak 15.00 to 17.30 (starting even earlier on some lines on Friday afternoons). The most frequent peak services are every 3 minutes on lines U6 and U9, and the combined service on U1 and U15 between Wittenbergplatz and Warschauer Strasse. Lines U2, U5 (Alexanderplatz to Kaulsdorf Nord) and U7 (Rudow to Rohrdamm) have a peak service of 3-3½ minutes (three trains every 10 minutes). Lines U4 and U8 have 5-minute peak services (and also U7 between Rohrdamm and Rathaus Spandau), while U1 and U15 at their western ends are every 6 minutes and U5 to Hönow every 6-7 minutes. Akin with Paris, the evening service intervals are the same every day of the year (but in Berlin 10 minutes on every line) although the finishing times vary at weekends as hitherto described.

On the U-Bahn, train departures at staff-attended stations are indicated by a white flashing light under the starting signal. On the open sections of line U5 and at some stations on the S-Bahn, indication is given in two visual stages – a white horizontal bar (to close the doors) and a vertical green bar (to depart). This sequence is depicted at Wuhletal on 30 June 1995. *Brian Hardy*

The opulence of Rathaus Spandau on U7 is seen here, with a two-car set of F.79/1 stock (2650-2651) in the station after uncoupling operations on 23 June 1993. *Steve Williams*

When the two disconnected sections of U2 were linked on 13 November 1993, the operation of line U1 was changed to run between Schlesisches Tor and Krumme Lanke, instead of being a shuttle from Wittenbergplatz to the latter. At the same time, line U3 was altered to become U15 and was extended to Schlesisches Tor (peaks) or Kottbusser Tor. A four-car set of A3 stock leads at Gleisdreieck. *Brian Hardy*

Trains For Service – Locations

The Note * indicates that the relevant depot or siding has trains from other lines starting/stabling as well.

Small Profile Lines

Line U1 – 15 trains:

4	Krumme Lanke
2	Breitenbachplatz
1	Fehrbelliner Platz *
2	Grunewald depot *
2	Nollendorfplatz *
1	Warschauer Strasse
3	Warschauer Strasse depot *

Line U15 – 9 trains:

1	Gleisdreieck
4	Uhlandstrasse
1	Spichernstrasse
1	Grunewald depot *
1	Fehrbelliner Platz *
1	Warschauer Strasse depot *

Line U2 – 31 trains:

12	Grunewald depot *
2	Zoologischer Garten
8	Vinetastrasse
1	Spittelmarkt
2	Alexanderplatz
1	Potsdamer Platz
1	Neu-Westend
2	Theodor-Heuss-Platz
1	Deutsche Oper
1	Ruhleben

Line U4 – 4 trains:

3	Nollendorfplatz *
1	Innsbrucker Platz

Line U4, operated with four two-car trains daily, was originally operated independently by the Schöneberg U-Bahn. *Capital Transport*

Large Profile Lines

Line U5 – 24 trains:

3	Hönow station
7	Hönow sidings
2	Kaulsdorf-Nord
1	Biesdorf-Süd
3	Tierpark
2	Frankfurter Allee
2	Friedrichsfelde depot
4	Alexanderplatz

Line 7 – 39 trains:

4	Richard-Wagner-Platz
3	Hermannplatz (lower)
2	Hermannplatz (upper)
4	Rohrdamm
4	Fehrbelliner Platz
6	Rathaus Spandau
1	Jakob-Kaiser-Platz
3	Grenzallee
3	Britz-Süd sidings
4	Britz depot
5	Rudow

Line U9 – 19 trains:

5	Osloer Strasse *
5	Rathaus Steglitz
4	Leopoldplatz
3	Zoologischer Garten
1	Seestrasse depot *
1	Walther-Schreiber-Platz

Line U6 – 31 trains:

4	Tempelhof (Südring)
1	Hallesches Tor
8	Alt-Mariendorf
2	Platz der Luftbrücke
4	Kurt-Schumacher-Platz
6	Alt-Tegel
4	Seestrasse depot / sidings
2	Wedding

Line U8 – 18 trains:

3	Leinestrasse
2	Osloer Strasse *
2	Paracelsus-Bad
2	Gesundbrunnen
3	Boddinstrasse
6	Wittenau

A feature of the Berlin U-Bahn is that (on all lines except U8 and U9), stations are 'manned' during operational hours. A member of staff is located in a room, generally in the middle of the platform, having visible access or CCTV to both platforms (at stations with 'side' platforms, there may be a member of staff on each at busy times, or one member of staff may control both platforms with CCTV for the other). Announcements are made over the public address system, announcing the station name and the departure of the train. The station staff then give a 'right' indication to the driver by operating a button, which in turn illuminates a white flashing light beneath the station starting signal. For this reason therefore, two trains together in a station at an island platform are unlikely to start up simultaneously. It is interesting to note that on the former 'closed' stations in East Berlin, the observation accommodation for station staff remains just a simple 'pedestal' with the public address and signal to start.

On lines U8 and U9, OPO mirrors and CCTV monitors have displaced the Station Attendants, freeing them to concentrate on station and passenger matters. Line U1 is expected to follow suit in the near future.

U-Bahn Depots

Grunewald
This depot serves all small profile stock on all such lines and is located adjacent to and north west of Olympia-Stadion (Ost) station. It was first opened in 1912 and more recently in 1984/85 it has been enlarged. In addition to the four separate workshop buildings (two for maintenance and two for repairs), there is also a fifth four-track shed just north-west of the station between the running lines. Engineers trains and vehicles are also stabled here, often alongside the line in the outbound direction.

Zehlendorf
This depot is located at Krumme Lanke and was first provided in 1929 for the southern extension of what is now line U1 from Thielplatz. Here, there are four covered eight-car tracks and one open siding on each side of the shed. It is located north-east of the station on the south side of the line. Since 1 May 1968 it has been used only for light maintenance.

Seestrasse
Seestrasse was the first depot built for large profile rolling stock between 1919 and 1927, opening in 1923. There were originally 16 tracks for 96 cars and it currently maintains the 'D' and 'F' stocks on lines U6, U8 and U9. There are now two covered roads for heavy repairs and 19 roads for maintenance.

Friedrichsfelde
Opened in 1930 for what is now line U5, this depot also maintained the small profile stock during "Berlin Wall" years, operating on what is now the northern section of line U2. There were originally six tracks, each for six cars, plus six service tracks. There are now 13 covered roads and even more sidings.

Britz
This depot opened in 1965 and serves the large number of trains on line U7, the U-Bahn's longest operational line. It comprises 14 covered tracks and many open-air sidings.

Hönow
Although not a 'depot' in its own right, there are a large number of open-air stabling sidings, provided from 1989 with the north-east extension of line E, now line U5.

Warschauer Strasse
This was the original depot built in 1900-01 by Siemens and Halske AG for U-Bahn trains and opened in 1902. It comprised four tracks for 32 cars. Closed and abandoned overnight on 13 August 1961 as a result of the Berlin Wall, this four-track depot reopened on 14 October 1995 at the same time as line U1 was extended from Schlesisches Tor to Warschauer Strasse. A second building on the east side of the station for eight tracks is currently under construction for opening in late-1996.

Grunewald depot maintains all of the U-Bahn narrow profile stock. On the left is a motor car of A3.66 stock and on the right A3L.67. Note the waist-level beading on motor car 914, a feature which has since been removed from all A3 stock and its large profile D stock counterparts.
Bob Greenaway

Closed Depots

Gleisdreieck
This depot, in the triangular junction of the original lines, was built by Siemens and Halske AG in 1901. It closed in 1912 as a result of the reconstruction of the track layout in the area and the provision of a new two-level station.

Schöneberg
Comprising five tracks, this depot was built for the then independent Schöneberger U-Bahn and was situated south of the terminus at Innsbrucker Platz in Eisackstrasse. When the line passed to the Hochbahn in 1926 the depot became superfluous and closed in 1930 (although some sources state 1935). All traces of this small depot were obliterated by air raid damage in 1943.

Thielplatz
Provided in 1913 for when what is now line U1 was a shuttle between Fehrbelliner Platz and Thielplatz, this small depot comprised three tracks. The extension southwestwards to Krumme Lanke (and a new depot built there) rendered it unnecessary and it closed in 1930, being finally demolished in 1960.

U-Bahn Fares And Tickets

Fares on the U-Bahn were originally based on the number of stations passed during a single journey. These, therefore, varied from 10 Pf in third class for four stations, to 30 Pf for a journey covering the entire system. Second class fares were in every case slightly dearer and ranged from 15 Pf to 40 Pf. Cheaper early morning fares were also available. For comparison it should be mentioned that the trams had at this time a flat fare of 10 Pf. On 3 November 1912, the number of stations in each fare band was slightly increased. On the Schöneberg line until 1918, fares were 15 Pf and 20 Pf, but each ticket allowed two journeys. Standard Edmondson card tickets were used.

On 1 April 1918 the number of fares was reduced to four, with an increase in the basic third class fare to 15 Pf and the number was again cut to three on 23 January 1919, when the early morning fares were abolished. On New Year's Day 1920, the number of fares was reduced to two – a short trip (five stations) for 30 Pf (third class) and 40 Pf for any longer journey. Probably at this time there was a change to paper tickets.

Thereafter, fares increased rapidly as inflation gathered speed and there would be no point in listing each change. When the Mark was stablised again on 22 November 1923, fares were fixed at 10 Pf for five stations and 15 Pf for longer journeys in third class. These were further increased to 15 Pf and 20 Pf respectively on 20 March 1925. After the City of Berlin acquired the share capital of the Hochbahn in July 1926, it was decided to introduce common fare structure for all forms of transport and on 15 March 1927, second class was abolished and a flat fare of 20 Pf was instituted. The basic fare allowed one transfer to or from trams. Transfer to or from the suburban railways, soon to become the S-Bahn, at a fare of 30 Pf was instituted on 1 January 1928, from which date a transfer to or from buses was also allowed. Later, from 2 July 1930, this also commanded a surcharge. The basic fare was increased to 25 Pf on 2 January 1930. During the period of economic and social unrest of the early-1930s, there was considerable abuse of the transfer facility and some unemployed people began to eke out a living by picking up discarded tickets which still had a valid transfer and selling these to prospective passengers for a small consideration – in return the duration of the validity was reduced to one hour from the start of a journey and checks at exchange points were stepped up, until fraud was reduced to 'acceptable' proportions again. The charge for any transfer was also raised to 30 Pf on 1 September 1931, when a five-journey "Sammelkarte" (without transfer) was also introduced, at a cost of RM 1. The basic fare, by government decree, again allowed one transfer between trams and U-Bahn from 1 January 1932, when the price of the multi-journey became 90 Pf.

A short trip fare of 10 Pf for three stations was available from 1 September 1933 and a further grade of 15 Pf for five stations was instituted on 1 October 1937. Season tickets for trams and U-Bahn were also reintroduced then. The Olympic Games of 1936 had seen the introduction of the first one-day and ten-day tourist tickets, for RM 1.50 and RM 13.50 respectively. Berliners took great advantage of the short journey fares and in 1939 some 66% of all journeys were made on such tickets.

A war tariff was brought into operation on 1 September 1944 and this had a flat fare of 20 Pf, with no transfer. An eight-journey ticket cost RM 1 and a limited number of season tickets remained available. Just before the end of the war, when services were under great pressure at peak times, a special 'permission to travel' ticket was introduced for U- and S-Bahn journeys at all times of the day from 8 April 1945. These were issued for journeys to and from work, for journeys connected with the war effort and for single trips for which permission had been obtained from the local police, this being granted only on proof of necessity, such as a medical appointment letter. Journeys of less than 3 km were to be made on foot. Soon, however, there were no trains to travel on, for any journey.

When services began again, only the basic 20 Pf fare was available, and without transfer. Five-journey tickets were available again from 1 May 1946 at a cost of RM 1.

The currency reforms of 1948 brought incredible difficulties for the BVG, at that time still functioning as a unitary undertaking. Initially, East and West Marks were at par and both were valid in all parts of Berlin and the inconvenience was limited to working in two currencies. Soon, however, the East Mark went down in value to about 25 Pf of the DM and naturally most passengers paid in East Marks! Until 28 March 1949, BVG had to put up with this, but on that date, with the agreement of the western powers, journeys which began in the western sectors had to be paid for in DM, while those in the Russian sector had to be paid for in mark.

Fares in West Berlin were first increased (to 25 Pf) in May 1951 and thereafter, as deficits grew, at regular intervals, although transfer to other BVG services was allowed from 1 March 1976, by which date the fare was DM 1. From the mid-1960s onwards, there was considerable mechanisation of ticket issue, in the interests of reducing labour costs and most tickets, which are of the thin card type, are now obtained from machines.

The basic fare in East Berlin remained at 20 Pf, with a five-journey ticket for M 1, until after reunification. Some season tickets were also available and, latterly, tourist tickets, at a cost of M 1 for one day (M 2 with the S-Bahn), were also issued. Holders of season or tourist tickets were expected to hold these up for inspection by other passengers when entering a platform. Single tickets, printed on flimsy grey paper, were validated by insertion into a rather basic canceller before beginning a journey.

Soon after the opening of the frontier, on 1 January 1990, BVG and BVB began to work towards a common tariff, while at the same time, the right to free travel on BVG transport for citizens of the DDR – in practice, almost entirely pensioners – was abolished. The main difficulty was the assimilation of a very cheap, though rather inflexible fare structure with one at a much higher level, with a much wider range of options. From 1991 there were effectively two tariffs in operation on both systems, one for visitors and residents of what had been West Berlin and a cheaper tariff for those resident in the former DDR at the time of reunification. Despite the availability of the cheaper tariff, known as tariff B, there have inevitably been considerable fare increases for passengers in the eastern part of Berlin. The main increase was made on 1 August 1991 when the BVB basic fare went from 20 Pf to DEM 1 in one leap, even although this was still only half the BVG fare. Successive increases have narrowed the differences.

At the time of writing the basic fare is DEM 3.70 and this allows unlimited travel on any form of transport within the Verkehrsbund Berlin-Brandenburg for two hours. Tickets may be bought at any time for later use, but must be cancelled before the journey actually begins. A short-journey fare of DEM 2.50 allows travel between a maximum of three stations, but carries no right of transfer to bus or tram. A Sammel-karte (four-journey) ticket is available for DEM 12.50 but visitors may find either the 30-hour ticket at DEM 15 or the seven-day ticket at DEM 40, a better bargain. Those staying longer than a week should obtain an Umweltkarte (Environment Ticket) which costs DEM 89 for one calendar month or DEM 760 for one year. Both seven-day and the Umweltkarte are transferable.

For persons who were resident in the DDR on 3 October 1990, tariff B is still available but only for seasonal cards (Umweltkarte; Wochenkarte).

Appendix One: Preserved Rolling Stock

As is often the case with trains replaced by more modern stock, much of it goes to the scrapyard. A lesser number survive to be used for less glamorous engineering and other miscellaneous duties and only a very few are fortunate enough to be kept for posterity.

Some small profile vehicles were taken to the high level station at Nollendorfplatz for the flea market, selling an enormous variety of items and providing refreshments. There were 16 such cars, all of class A2 of 1928-29 vintage and comprised motor cars 381 and 400, and trailers 776, 777, 781, 787, 789, 791, 806, 817, 818, 821, 826, 835, 857 and 861.

A further two motor coaches of wide profile C2 stock (cars 1314 and 1364 of 1929-30 origin) were used at the Turkish bazaar at Bülowstrasse as toilets.

Other vehicles which have survived, can be summarised as follows:

Museum für Verkehr und Technik, Berlin:

No	Gauge	Class	Type
35	Large profile	B1	Motor
118	Large profile	B2	Motor
559	Small profile	A1	Trailer
1352	Large profile	C	Motor
1804	Large profile	E3/1	Motor
1805	Large profile	E3/1	Trailer

Owned by BVG – Museum Trains:

No	Gauge	Class	Type
7	Small profile	A1	Motor
31	Small profile	A1	Motor
722	Small profile	A1	Trailer
737	Small profile	A1	Trailer
390	Small profile	A2	Motor
425	Small profile	A2	Motor
836	Small profile	A2	Trailer
848	Small profile	A2	Trailer
26	Large profile	B1	Motor
66	Large profile	B1	Motor
320	Large profile	B1	Trailer
113	Large profile	B2	Trailer
131	Large profile	B2	Motor
299	Large profile	B2	Trailer
358	Large profile	B2	Trailer

Owned by BVG – Stored

No	Gauge	Class	Type	Notes
86	Small profile	A1	Motor	ex–125.458
262	Small profile	A1	Motor	ex–125.438
294	Small profile	A1	Motor	ex–125.448
515	Small profile	A1	Trailer	
753	Small profile	A1	Trailer	ex–175.443
310	Small profile	A2.U	Motor	ex–128.700
312	Small profile	A2.U	Motor	ex–128.736
377	Small profile	A2	Motor	ex–127.618
385	Small profile	A2	Motor	ex–127.622
390	Small profile	A2	Motor	

No	Gauge	Class	Type	Notes
404	Small profile	A2	Motor	ex–127.638
425	Small profile	A2	Motor	
809	Small profile	A2.U	Trailer	ex–178.737
836	Small profile	A2	Trailer	
848	Small profile	A2	Trailer	
851	Small profile	A2	Trailer	ex–177.623
1316	Large profile	C2	Trailer	ex–563
1338	Large profile	C2	Trailer	ex–588
1382	Large profile	C2	Trailer	ex–652
1816	Large profile	E3/1	Motor	ex–101.016
1817	Large profile	E3/1	Trailer	
1880	Large profile	E3/3	Motor	ex–103.080
1881	Large profile	E3/3	Trailer	ex–153.081
1914	Large profile	E3/5	Motor	ex–105.114
1915	Large profile	E3/5	Trailer	ex–155.115

Other withdrawn U-Bahn stock can be found, as follows:

Small Profile:

No.	Class	Type	Location
12	A1	Motor	Klosterstrasse, line U2, cab end and part of car in wall of station platform level at north end. This car was one from the Schöneberg U-Bahn.
32	A1	Motor	Hummelbahn, Hamburg.
56	A1.U	Motor	Boutique adjacent to Königs Wusterhausen station on line S46, now bears the number 512, which is not its original.
201	A1	Motor	Verkehrs Museum, Nürnberg.
345	A2	Motor	Osthavelländische Eisenbahn, Johannesstift.
382	A2	Motor	Diakoniezentrum, Heiligensee.
592	A1.U	Trailer	Boutique adjacent to Königs Wusterhausen station on line S46.
715	A1	Trailer	Boutique adjacent to Zeuthen station on lines S6 and S46, selling jeans.
733	A1	Trailer	Boutique adjacent to Zeuthen station on lines S6 and S46, selling jeans.
747	A1	Trailer	Hummelbahn, Hamburg.
755	A1	Trailer	Diakoniezentrum, Heiligensee.
792	A2	Trailer	Kindertagesstätte, Paul-Lincke-Ufer Ecke Lausitzer Strasse.
814	A2	Trailer	Dresden, Maystrasse.
816	A2	Trailer	Construction company, Peter Grosse, Saatwinkler Damm.
820	A2	Trailer	Ausschankstube Turnverein TSC 1893 Grenzalleebrücke – café.
833	A2	Trailer	Abenteuerspielplatz, Jungfernheide.
846	A2	Trailer	Lagerraum für Gartenbauamt Buschkrugallee Ecke Hannemannstrasse.
855	A2	Trailer	Diakoniezentrum, Heiligensee.

Large Profile:

No.	Class	Type	Location
115	B2	Motor	Daimler-Benz-Niederlassung Salzufer.
128	B2	Motor	Berliner Eisenbahnfreunde Waldstrasse.
133	B2	Motor	Tennishalle Sangerhauser Weg.
233	B1	Motor	Diakoniezentrum, Heiligensee.
293	B1	Trailer	Diakoniezentrum, Heiligensee.
298	B2	Trailer	Diakoniezentrum, Heiligensee.
1308	C2	Motor	Berliner Eisenbahnfreunde.
1310	C2	Motor	Polizeikaserne Kruppstrasse, as café.
1332	C2	Motor	Berliner Eisenbahnfreunde.

Appendix Two: U-Bahn Rolling Stock List

D Stock Train Formations

Former Numbers	Motor	Motor	Former Numbers	Line	Type	Built By	Year
	2000	2001		5	D.56	O&K	1956
110.300	2002	2003	110.301	7	D.57	O&K	1957–58
110.302	2004	2005	110.303	5	D.57	O&K	1957–58
110.304	2006	2007	110.305	5	D.57	O&K	1957–58
110.306	2008	2009	110.307	5	D.57	O&K	1957–58
110.308	2010	2011	110.309	5	D.57	O&K	1957–58
110.310	2012	2013	110.311	7	D.57	O&K	1957–58
110.312	2014	2015	110.313	7	D.57	O&K	1957–58
110.314	2016	2017	110.315	7	D.57	O&K	1957–58
110.316	2018	2019	110.317	5	D.57	O&K	1957–58
	2020	2021		7	D.57	O&K	1957
110.318	2022	2023	110.319	7	D.57	O&K	1957–58
110.320	2024	2025	110.321	7	D.57	O&K	1957–58
110.322	2026	2027	110.323	5	D.57	O&K	1957–58
110.324	2028	2029	110.325	5	D.57	DWM	1957–58
110.326	2030	2031	110.327	5	D.57	DWM	1957–58
110.328	2032	2033	110.329	5	D.57	DWM	1957–58
110.330	2034	2035	110.331	5	D.57	DWM	1957–58
110.332	2036	2037	110.333	5	D.57	DWM	1957–58
110.334	2038	2039	110.335	5	D.57	DWM	1957–58
110.336	2040	2041	110.337	5	D.57	DWM	1957–58
110.338	2042	2043	110.339	5	D.57	DWM	1957–58
110.340	2044	2045	110.341	5	D.57	DWM	1957–58
110.342	2046	2047	110.343	5	D.57	DWM	1957–58
110.344	2048	2049	110.345	5	D.57	DWM	1957–58
110.348	2052	2053	110.349	7	D.57	DWM	1957–58
	2054	2055		6	D.60	O&K	1960–61
	2056	2057		6	D.60	O&K	1960–61
	2058	2059		6	D.60	O&K	1960–61
110.350	2060	2061	110.351	5	D.60	O&K	1960–61
110.352	2062	2063	110.353	6	D.60	O&K	1960–61
110.354	2064	2065	110.355	5	D.60	O&K	1960–61
110.356	2066	2067	110.357	6	D.60	O&K	1960–61
110.358	2068	2069	110.359	5	D.60	O&K	1960–61
110.360	2070	2071	110.361	5	D.60	O&K	1960–61
	2072	2073		6	D.60	O&K	1960–61

Former Numbers	Motor	Motor	Former Numbers	Line	Type	Built By	Year
110.364	2074	2075	110.365	5	D.60	O&K	1960–61
	2076	2077		6	D.60	O&K	1960–61
110.368	2078	2079	110.369	5	D.60	O&K	1960–61
110.370	2080	2081	110.371	5	D.60	O&K	1960–61
110.372	2082	2083	110.373	6	D.60	O&K	1960–61
110.374	2084	2085	110.375	5	D.60	DWM	1960–61
110.376	2086	2087	110.377	6	D.60	DWM	1960–61
110.378	2088	2089	110.379	6	D.60	DWM	1960–61
	2090	2091		6	D.60	DWM	1960–61
	2092	2093		6	D.60	DWM	1960–61
	2094	2095		6	D.60	DWM	1960–61
110.386	2096	2097	110.387	6	D.60	DWM	1960–61
110.388	2098	2099	110.389	6	D.60	DWM	1960–61
	2100	2101		5	D.60	DWM	1960–61
110.390	2102	2103	110.391	7	D.60	DWM	1960–61
110.392	2104	2105	110.393	7	D.60	DWM	1960–61
110.394	2106	2107	110.395	7	D.60	DWM	1960–61
110.396	2108	2109	110.397	7	D.60	DWM	1960–61
110.398	2110	2111	110.399	7	D.60	DWM	1960–61
110.400	2112	2113	110.401	7	D.60	DWM	1960–61

Motor	Motor	Line	Type	Built By	Year	Motor	Motor	Line	Type	Built By	Year
2114	2115	7	D.63	O&K	1963–64	2160	2161	7	D.63	DWM	1963–64
2116	2117	7	D.63	O&K	1963–64	2162	2163	7	D.63	DWM	1963–64
2118	2119	7	D.63	O&K	1963–64	2164	2165	7	D.63	DWM	1963–64
2120	2121	7	D.63	O&K	1963–64	2166	2167	7	D.63	DWM	1963–64
2122	2123	7	D.63	O&K	1963–64	2168	2169	7	D.63	DWM	1963–64
2124	2125	7	D.63	O&K	1963–64	2170	2171	7	D.63	DWM	1963–64
2126	2127	7	D.63	O&K	1963–64	2172	2173	7	D.63	DWM	1963–64
2128	2129	7	D.63	O&K	1963–64	2174	2175	7	D.63	DWM	1963–64
2130	2131	7	D.63	O&K	1963–64	2176	2177	7	D.63	DWM	1963–64
2132	2133	7	D.63	O&K	1963–64	2178	2179	7	D.63	DWM	1963–64
2134	2135	7	D.63	O&K	1963–64	2180	2181	7	D.63	DWM	1963–64
2136	2137	7	D.63	O&K	1963–64	2182	2183	7	D.63	DWM	1963–64
2138	2139	7	D.63	O&K	1963–64	2184	2185	7	D.63	DWM	1963–64
2140	2141	7	D.63	O&K	1963–64	2186	2187	7	D.65	O&K	1965
2142	2143	7	D.63	O&K	1963–64	2188	2189	7	D.65	O&K	1965
2144	2145	7	D.63	O&K	1963–64	2190	2191	7	D.65	O&K	1965
2146	2147	7	D.63	O&K	1963–64	2192	2193	7	D.65	O&K	1965
2148	2149	7	D.63	O&K	1963–64	2194	2195	7	D.65	O&K	1965
2150	2151	7	D.63	DWM	1963–64	2196	2197	7	D.65	O&K	1965
2152	2153	7	D.63	DWM	1963–64	2198	2199	7	D.65	O&K	1965
2154	2155	7	D.63	DWM	1963–64	2200	2201	6	D.65	O&K	1965
2156	2157	7	D.63	DWM	1963–64	2202	2203	7	D.65	O&K	1965
2158	2159	7	D.63	DWM	1963–64	2204	2205	7	D.65	O&K	1965

Motor	Motor	Line	Type	Built By	Year	Motor	Motor	Line	Type	Built By	Year
2206	2207	7	D.65	O&K	1965	2300	2301	5	DL.68	O&K	1968–70
2208	2209	7	D.65	O&K	1965	2302	2303	6	DL.68	O&K	1968–70
2210	2211	7	D.65	O&K	1965	2304	2305	5	DL.68	DWM	1968–70
2212	2213	7	D.65	O&K	1965	2306	2307	5	DL.68	DWM	1968–70
2214	2215	7	D.65	O&K	1965	2308	2309	5	DL.68	DWM	1968–70
2216	2217	7	D.65	O&K	1965	2310	2311	5	DL.68	DWM	1968–70
2218	2219	7	D.65	O&K	1965	2312	2313	5	DL.68	DWM	1968–70
2220	2221	7	D.65	O&K	1965	2314	2315	6	DL.68	DWM	1968–70
2222	2223	7	D.65	O&K	1965	2316	2317	5	DL.68	DWM	1968–70
2224	2225	7	D.65	O&K	1965	2318	2319	5	DL.68	DWM	1968–70
2226	2227	7	D.65	O&K	1965	2320	2321	5	DL.68	DWM	1968–70
2228	2229	7	D.65	O&K	1965	2322	2323	5	DL.68	DWM	1968–70
2230	2231	6	DL.65	O&K	1965–66	2324	2325	5	DL.68	DWM	1968–70
2232	2233	6	DL.65	O&K	1965–66	2326	2327	5	DL.68	DWM	1968–70
2234	2235	6	DL.65	O&K	1965–66	2328	2329	5	DL.68	DWM	1968–70
2236	2237	5	DL.68	O&K	1968–70	2330	2331	5	DL.68	DWM	1968–70
2238	2239	5	DL.68	O&K	1968–70	2332	2333	5	DL.68	DWM	1968–70
2240	2241	5	DL.68	O&K	1968–70	2334	2335	5	DL.68	DWM	1968–70
2242	2243	5	DL.68	O&K	1968–70	2336	2337	5	DL.68	DWM	1968–70
2244	2245	5	DL.68	O&K	1968–70	2338	2339	5	DL.68	DWM	1968–70
2246	2247	5	DL.68	O&K	1968–70	2340	2341	5	DL.68	DWM	1968–70
2248	2249	6	DL.68	O&K	1968–70	2342	2343	5	DL.68	DWM	1968–70
2250	2251	6	DL.68	O&K	1968–70	2344	2345	5	DL.68	DWM	1968–70
2252	2253	5	DL.68	O&K	1968–70	2346	2347	5	DL.68	DWM	1968–70
2254	2255	5	DL.68	O&K	1968–70	2348	2349	5	DL.68	DWM	1968–70
2256	2257	5	DL.68	O&K	1968–70	2350	2351	6	DL.68	DWM	1968–70
2258	2259	5	DL.68	O&K	1968–70	2352	2353	6	DL.68	DWM	1968–70
2260	2261	5	DL.68	O&K	1968–70	2354	2355	5	DL.68	DWM	1968–70
2262	2263	6	DL.68	O&K	1968–70	2356	2357	5	DL.68	DWM	1968–70
2264	2265	5	DL.68	O&K	1968–70	2358	2359	5	DL.68	DWM	1968–70
2266	2267	5	DL.68	O&K	1968–70	2360	2361	5	DL.68	DWM	1968–70
2268	2269	5	DL.68	O&K	1968–70	2362	2363	5	DL.68	DWM	1968–70
2270	2271	6	DL.68	O&K	1968–70	2364	2365	5	DL.68	DWM	1968–70
2272	2273	5	DL.68	O&K	1968–70	2366	2367	5	DL.68	DWM	1968–70
2274	2275	5	DL.68	O&K	1968–70	2368	2369	5	DL.68	DWM	1968–70
2276	2277	5	DL.68	O&K	1968–70	2370	2371	5	DL.68	DWM	1968–70
2278	2279	5	DL.68	O&K	1968–70	2372	2373	5	DL.70	O&K	1970–71
2280	2281	5	DL.68	O&K	1968–70	2374	2375	5	DL.70	O&K	1970–71
2282	2283	5	DL.68	O&K	1968–70	2376	2377	5	DL.70	O&K	1970–71
2284	2285	5	DL.68	O&K	1968–70	2378	2379	5	DL.70	O&K	1970–71
2286	2287	5	DL.68	O&K	1968–70	2380	2381	5	DL.70	O&K	1970–71
2288	2289	5	DL.68	O&K	1968–70	2382	2383	5	DL.70	O&K	1970–71
2290	2291	6	DL.68	O&K	1968–70	2384	2385	5	DL.70	O&K	1970–71
2292	2293	5	DL.68	O&K	1968–70	2386	2387	5	DL.70	O&K	1970–71
2294	2295	5	DL.68	O&K	1968–70	2388	2389	5	DL.70	O&K	1970–71
2296	2297	5	DL.68	O&K	1968–70	2390	2391	5	DL.70	O&K	1970–71
2298	2299	5	DL.68	O&K	1968–70	2392	2393	6	DL.70	O&K	1970–71

Motor	Motor	Line	Type	Built By	Year	Motor	Motor	Line	Type	Built By	Year
2394	2395	6	DL.70	O&K	1970–71	2414	2415	6	DL.70	O&K	1970–71
2396	2397	6	DL.70	O&K	1970–71	2416	2417	6	DL.70	O&K	1970–71
2398	2399	6	DL.70	O&K	1970–71	2418	2419	6	DL.70	O&K	1970–71
2400	2401	5	DL.70	O&K	1970–71	2420	2421	6	DL.70	O&K	1970–71
2402	2403	6	DL.70	O&K	1970–71	2422	2423	6	DL.70	O&K	1970–71
2404	2405	6	DL.70	O&K	1970–71	2424	2425	6	DL.70	O&K	1970–71
2406	2407	6	DL.70	O&K	1970–71	2426	2427	6	DL.70	O&K	1970–71
2408	2409	6	DL.70	O&K	1970–71	2428	2429	6	DL.70	O&K	1970–71
2410	2411	6	DL.70	O&K	1970–71	2430	2431	6	DL.70	O&K	1970–71
2412	2413	6	DL.70	O&K	1970–71						

A3 & A3L Type Train Formations
Lines U1, U2, U4 (shown *) and U15

Motor	Motor	Type	Built By	Year	Motor	Motor	Type	Built By	Year
656	657	A3L.71	O&K	1972–73	720	721	A3L.71	O&K	1972–73
658	659	A3L.71	O&K	1972–73	722	723	A3L.71	O&K	1972–73
660	661	A3L.71	O&K	1972–73	724	725	A3L.71	O&K	1972–73
662	663	A3L.71	O&K	1972–73	726	727	A3L.71	O&K	1972–73
664	665	A3L.71	O&K	1972–73	728	729	A3L.71	O&K	1972–73
666	667	A3L.71	O&K	1972–73	730	731	A3L.71	O&K	1972–73
668	669	A3L.71	O&K	1972–73	732	733	A3L.71	O&K	1972–73
670	671	A3L.71	O&K	1972–73	734	735	A3L.71	O&K	1972–73
672	673	A3L.71	O&K	1972–73	736	737	A3L.71	O&K	1972–73
674	675	A3L.71	O&K	1972–73	738	739	A3L.71	O&K	1972–73
676	677	A3L.71	O&K	1972–73	740	741	A3L.71	O&K	1972–73
678	679	A3L.71	O&K	1972–73	742	743	A3L.71	O&K	1972–73
680	681	A3L.71	O&K	1972–73	744	745	A3L.71	O&K	1972–73
682*	683*	A3L.71	O&K	1972–73	746	747	A3L.71	O&K	1972–73
684	685	A3L.71	O&K	1972–73	748*	749*	A3L.71	O&K	1972–73
686	687	A3L.71	O&K	1972–73	750	751	A3L.71	O&K	1972–73
688*	689	A3L.71	O&K	1972–73	752	753	A3L.71	O&K	1972–73
690*	691*	A3L.71	O&K	1972–73	754	755	A3L.71	O&K	1972–73
692*	693*	A3L.71	O&K	1972–73	756	757	A3L.71	O&K	1972–73
694	695	A3L.71	O&K	1972–73	758	759	A3L.71	O&K	1972–73
696	697	A3L.71	O&K	1972–73	760	761	A3L.71	O&K	1972–73
698	699	A3L.71	O&K	1972–73	762	763	A3L.71	O&K	1972–73
700*	701*	A3L.71	O&K	1972–73	764	765	A3L.71	O&K	1972–73
702*	703*	A3L.71	O&K	1972–73	766	767	A3L.71	O&K	1972–73
704	705	A3L.71	O&K	1972–73	768	769	A3L.71	O&K	1972–73
706*	707	A3L.71	O&K	1972–73	770	771	A3L.71	O&K	1972–73
708	709	A3L.71	O&K	1972–73	772	773	A3L.71	O&K	1972–73
710	711	A3L.71	O&K	1972–73	774	775	A3L.71	O&K	1972–73
712	713	A3L.71	O&K	1972–73	776	777	A3L.71	O&K	1972–73
714	715	A3L.71	O&K	1972–73	778	779	A3L.71	O&K	1972–73
716*	717	A3L.71	O&K	1972–73	780	781	A3L.71	O&K	1972–73
718*	719	A3L.71	O&K	1972–73	782	783	A3L.71	O&K	1972–73

Motor	Motor	Type	Built By	Year	Motor	Motor	Type	Built By	Year
784	785	A3L.71	O&K	1972–73	882	883	A3L.67	O&K	1967–68
786	787	A3L.71	O&K	1972–73	884	885	A3L.66	O&K	1966
788	789	A3L.71	O&K	1972–73	886	887	A3L.66	O&K	1966
790	791	A3L.71	O&K	1972–73	888	889	A3L.66	O&K	1966
792	793	A3L.71	O&K	1972–73	890	891	A3L.66	O&K	1966
794	795	A3L.67	O&K	1967–68	892	893	A3.66	O&K	1966
796	797	A3L.67	O&K	1967–68	894	895	A3.66	O&K	1966
798	799	A3L.67	O&K	1967–68	896	897	A3.66	O&K	1966
800	801	A3L.67	O&K	1967–68	898	899	A3.66	O&K	1966
802	803	A3L.67	O&K	1967–68	900	901	A3.66	O&K	1966
804	805	A3L.67	O&K	1967–68	902	903	A3.66	O&K	1966
806	807	A3L.67	O&K	1967–68	904	905	A3.66	O&K	1966
808	809	A3L.67	O&K	1967–68	906	907	A3.66	O&K	1966
810	811	A3L.67	O&K	1967–68	908	909	A3.66	O&K	1966
812	813	A3L.67	O&K	1967–68	910	911	A3.66	O&K	1966
814	815	A3L.67	O&K	1967–68	912	913	A3.66	DWM	1966
816	817	A3L.67	O&K	1967–68	914	915	A3.66	DWM	1966
818	819	A3L.67	O&K	1967–68	916	917	A3.66	DWM	1966
820	821	A3L.67	O&K	1967–68	918	919	A3.66	DWM	1966
822	823	A3L.67	O&K	1967–68	920	921	A3.66	DWM	1966
824	825	A3L.67	O&K	1967–68	922	923	A3.66	DWM	1966
826	827	A3L.67	O&K	1967–68	924	925	A3.66	DWM	1966
828	829	A3L.67	O&K	1967–68	926	927	A3.66	DWM	1966
830	831	A3L.67	O&K	1967–68	928	929	A3.66	DWM	1966
832	833	A3L.67	O&K	1967–68	930	931	A3.66	DWM	1966
834	835	A3L.67	O&K	1967–68	932	933	A3.66	DWM	1966
836	837	A3L.67	O&K	1967–68	934	935	A3.64	O&K	1964
838	839	A3L.67	O&K	1967–68	936	937	A3.64	O&K	1964
840	841	A3L.67	O&K	1967–68	938	939	A3.64	O&K	1964
842	843	A3L.67	O&K	1967–68	940	941	A3.64	O&K	1964
844	845	A3L.67	O&K	1967–68	942	943	A3.64	O&K	1964
846	847	A3L.67	O&K	1967–68	944	945	A3.64	O&K	1964
848	849	A3L.67	O&K	1967–68	946	947	A3.64	O&K	1964
850	851	A3L.67	O&K	1967–68	948	949	A3.64	O&K	1964
852	853	A3L.67	O&K	1967–68	950	951	A3.64	O&K	1964
854	855	A3L.67	O&K	1967–68	952	953	A3.64	O&K	1964
856	857	A3L.67	O&K	1967–68	954	955	A3.64	O&K	1964
858	859	A3L.67	O&K	1967–68	956	957	A3.64	O&K	1964
860	861	A3L.67	O&K	1967–68	958	959	A3.64	O&K	1964
862	863	A3L.67	O&K	1967–68	960	961	A3.64	O&K	1964
864	865	A3L.67	O&K	1967–68	962	963	A3.64	O&K	1964
866	867	A3L.67	O&K	1967–68	964	965	A3.64	O&K	1964
868	869	A3L.67	O&K	1967–68	966	967	A3.64	O&K	1964
870	871	A3L.67	O&K	1967–68	968	969	A3.64	O&K	1964
872	873	A3L.67	O&K	1967–68	970	971	A3.64	O&K	1964
874	875	A3L.67	O&K	1967–68	972	973	A3.64	O&K	1964
876	877	A3L.67	O&K	1967–68	974	975	A3.64	O&K	1964
878	879	A3L.67	O&K	1967–68	976	977	A3.64	O&K	1964
880	881	A3L.67	O&K	1967–68	978	979	A3.64	O&K	1964

Motor	Motor	Type	Built By	Year	Motor	Motor	Type	Built By	Year
980	981	A3.64	O&K	1964	990	991	A3.60	DWM	1960–61
982	983	A3.64	O&K	1964	992	993	A3.60	DWM	1960–61
984	985	A3.60	DWM	1960–61	994	995	A3.60	DWM	1960–61
986	987	A3.60	DWM	1960–61	996	997	A3.60	DWM	1960–61
988	989	A3.60	DWM	1960–61	998	999	A3.60	DWM	1960–61

F Stock Train Formations
2500-2501 to 2636-2637 and 2640-2641 to 2646-2647 are equipped for ATO – line U9.

Motor	Motor	Line	Type	Built By	Year	Motor	Motor	Line	Type	Built By	Year
2500	2501	9	F.74/0	O&K	1973	2570	2571	9	F.76	O&K	1976–78
2502	2503	9	F.74/1	O&K	1974–75	2572	2573	9	F.76	O&K	1976–78
2504	2505	9	F.74/1	O&K	1974–75	2574	2575	9	F.76	O&K	1976–78
2506	2507	9	F.74/1	O&K	1974–75	2576	2577	9	F.76	O&K	1976–78
2508	2509	9	F.74/1	O&K	1974–75	2578	2579	9	F.76	O&K	1976–78
2510	2511	9	F.74/1	O&K	1974–75	2580	2581	9	F.76	O&K	1976–78
2512	2513	9	F.74/1	O&K	1974–75	2582	2583	9	F.76	O&K	1976–78
2514	2515	9	F.74/1	O&K	1974–75	2584	2585	9	F.76	O&K	1976–78
2516	2517	9	F.74/1	O&K	1974–75	2586	2587	9	F.76	O&K	1976–78
2518	2519	9	F.74/1	O&K	1974–75	2588	2589	9	F.76	O&K	1976–78
2520	2521	9	F.74/1	O&K	1974–75	2590	2591	9	F.76	O&K	1976–78
2522	2523	9	F.74/1	O&K	1974–75	2592	2593	9	F.76	O&K	1976–78
2524	2525	9	F.74/1	O&K	1974–75	2594	2595	9	F.76	O&K	1976–78
2526	2527	9	F.74/1	O&K	1974–75	2596	2597	9	F.76	O&K	1976–78
2528	2529	9	F.74/1	O&K	1974–75	2598	2599	9	F.76	O&K	1976–78
2530	2531	9	F.74/2	O&K	1974–75	2600	2601	9	F.76	O&K	1976–78
2532	2533	9	F.74/2	O&K	1974–75	2602	2603	9	F.76	O&K	1976–78
2534	2535	9	F.74/2	O&K	1974–75	2604	2605	9	F.76	O&K	1976–78
2536	2537	9	F.74/2	O&K	1974–75	2606	2607	9	F.76	O&K	1976–78
2538	2539	9	F.74/2	O&K	1974–75	2608	2609	9	F.76	WU	1976–78
2540	2541	9	F.74/2	O&K	1974–75	2610	2611	9	F.76	WU	1976–78
2542	2543	9	F.74/2	O&K	1974–75	2612	2613	9	F.76	WU	1976–78
2544	2545	9	F.74/2	O&K	1974–75	2614	2615	9	F.76	WU	1976–78
2546	2547	9	F.74/2	O&K	1974–75	2616	2617	9	F.76	WU	1976–78
2548	2549	9	F.74/2	O&K	1974–75	2618	2619	9	F.76	WU	1976–78
2550	2551	9	F.74/3	O&K	1974–75	2620	2621	9	F.76	WU	1976–78
2552	2553	9	F.74/3	O&K	1974–75	2622	2623	9	F.76	WU	1976–78
2554	2555	9	F.74/3	O&K	1974–75	2624	2625	9	F.76	WU	1976–78
2556	2557	9	F.76	O&K	1976–78	2626	2627	9	F.76	WU	1976–78
2558	2559	9	F.76	O&K	1976–78	2628	2629	9	F.76	WU	1976–78
2560	2561	9	F.76	O&K	1976–78	2630	2631	9	F.76	WU	1976–78
2562	2563	9	F.76	O&K	1976–78	2632	2633	9	F.76	WU	1976–78
2564	2565	9	F.76	O&K	1976–78	2634	2635	9	F.76	WU	1976–78
2566	2567	9	F.76	O&K	1976–78	2636	2637	9	F.76	WU	1976–78
2568	2569	9	F.76	O&K	1976–78	2638	2639	6	F.79/1	WU	1980–81

Motor	Motor	Line	Type	Built By	Year	Motor	Motor	Line	Type	Built By	Year
2640	2641	9	F.79/1	WU	1980–81	2728	2729	7	F.84	WU	1984–85
2642	2643	9	F.79/1	WU	1980–81	2730	2731	7	F.84	WU	1984–85
2644	2645	9	F.79/1	WU	1980–81	2732	2733	7	F.84	WU	1984–85
2646	2647	9	F.79/1	WU	1980–81	2734	2735	7	F.84	WU	1984–85
2648	2649	6	F.79/1	WU	1980–81	2736	2737	7	F.84	WU	1984–85
2650	2651	6	F.79/1	WU	1980–81	2738	2739	7	F.84	WU	1984–85
2652	2653	6	F.79/1	WU	1980–81	2740	2741	7	F.84	WU	1984–85
2654	2655	6	F.79/1	WU	1980–81	2742	2743	7	F.84	WU	1984–85
2656	2657	6	F.79/1	WU	1980–81	2744	2745	7	F.84	WU	1984–85
2658	2659	6	F.79/1	WU	1980–81	2746	2747	7	F.84	WU	1984–85
2660	2661	6	F.79/1	WU	1980–81	2748	2749	7	F.84	WU	1984–85
2662	2663	6	F.79/1	WU	1980–81	2750	2751	7	F.84	WU	1984–85
2664	2665	6	F.79/1	WU	1980–81	2752	2753	7	F.84	WU	1984–85
2666	2667	6	F.79/1	WU	1980–81	2754	2755	7	F.84	WU	1984–85
2668	2669	6	F.79/1	WU	1980–81	2756	2757	7	F.84	WU	1984–85
2670	2671	7	F.79/1	WU	1980–81	2758	2759	7	F.84	WU	1984–85
2672	2673	6	F.79/2	O&K	1979–80	2760	2761	7	F.84	WU	1984–85
2674	2675	6	F.79/2	O&K	1979–80	2762	2763	7	F.84	WU	1984–85
2676	2677	6	F.79/2	O&K	1979–80	2764	2765	7	F.84	WU	1984–85
2678	2679	6	F.79/2	O&K	1979–80	2766	2767	7	F.84	WU	1984–85
2680	2681	6	F.79/2	O&K	1979–80	2768	2769	7	F.84	WU	1984–85
2682	2683	6	F.79/2	O&K	1979–80	2770	2771	7	F.84	WU	1984–85
2684	2685	6	F.79/2	O&K	1979–80	2772	2773	7	F.84	WU	1984–85
2686	2687	6	F.79/2	O&K	1979–80	2774	2775	7	F.84	WU	1984–85
2688	2689	6	F.79/2	O&K	1979–80	2776	2777	7	F.84	WU	1984–85
2690	2691	6	F.79/2	O&K	1979–80	2778	2779	7	F.84	WU	1984–85
2692	2693	6	F.79/2	O&K	1979–80	2780	2781	7	F.84	WU	1984–85
2694	2695	6	F.79/2	O&K	1979–80	2782	2783	7	F.84	WU	1984–85
2696	2697	6	F.79/2	O&K	1979–80	2784	2785	7	F.84	WU	1984–85
2698	2699	6	F.79/2	O&K	1979–80	2786	2787	7	F.84	WU	1984–85
2700	2701	6	F.79/2	O&K	1979–80	2788	2789	7	F.84	WU	1984–85
2702	2703	6	F.79/2	O&K	1979–80	2790	2791	7	F.84	WU	1984–85
2704	2705	6	F.79/2	O&K	1979–80	2792	2793	7	F.84	WU	1984–85
2706	2707	6	F.79/2	O&K	1979–80	2794	2795	7	F.84	WU	1984–85
2708	2709	6	F.79/2	O&K	1979–80	2796	2797	7	F.84	WU	1984–85
2710	2711	6	F.79/2	O&K	1979–80	2798	2799	7	F.84	WU	1984–85
2712	2713	7	F.79/3	O&K	1980–81	2800	2801	7	F.84	WU	1984–85
2714	2715	7	F.79/3	O&K	1980–81	2802	2803	7	F.87	WU	1986–87
2716	2717	7	F.79/3	O&K	1980–81	2804	2805	7	F.87	WU	1986–87
2718	2719	7	F.79/3	O&K	1980–81	2806	2807	7	F.87	WU	1986–87
2720	2721	7	F.79/3	O&K	1980–81	2808	2809	7	F.87	WU	1986–87
2722	2723	7	F.79/3	O&K	1980–81	2810	2811	7	F.87	WU	1986–87
2724	2725	7	F.84	WU	1984–85	2812	2813	7	F.87	WU	1986–87
2726	2727	7	F.84	WU	1984–85	2814	2815	7	F.87	WU	1986–87

Motor	Motor	Line	Type	Built By	Year	Motor	Motor	Line	Type	Built By	Year
2816	2817	7	F.87	WU	1986–87	2904	2905	8	F.92	WU	1992–93
2818	2819	7	F.87	WU	1986–87	2906	2907	8	F.92	WU	1992–93
2820	2821	7	F.87	WU	1986–87	2908	2909	8	F.92	WU	1992–93
2822	2823	7	F.87	WU	1986–87	2910	2911	8	F.92	WU	1992–93
2824	2825	7	F.87	WU	1986–87	2912	2913	8	F.92	WU	1992–93
2826	2827	7	F.87	WU	1986–87	2914	2915	8	F.92	WU	1992–93
2828	2829	7	F.87	WU	1986–87	2916	2917	8	F.92	WU	1992–93
2830	2831	7	F.87	WU	1986–87	2918	2919	8	F.92	WU	1992–93
2832	2833	7	F.87	WU	1986–87	2920	2921	8	F.92	WU	1992–93
2834	2835	7	F.87	WU	1986–87	2922	2923	8	F.92	WU	1992–93
2836	2837	7	F.87	WU	1986–87	2924	2925	8	F.92	WU	1992–93
2838	2839	7	F.87	WU	1986–87	2926	2927	8	F.92	WU	1992–93
2840	2841	7	F.87	WU	1986–87	2928	2929	8	F.92	WU	1992–93
2842	2843	7	F.87	WU	1986–87	2930	2931	8	F.92	WU	1992–93
2844	2845	7	F.90	WU	1991–92	2932	2933	8	F.92	WU	1992–93
2846	2847	7	F.90	WU	1991–92	2934	2935	8	F.92	WU	1992–93
2848	2849	7	F.90	WU	1991–92	2936	2937	8	F.92	WU	1992–93
2850	2851	7	F.90	WU	1991–92	2938	2939	8	F.92	WU	1992–93
2852	2853	7	F.90	WU	1991–92	2940	2941	8	F.92	WU	1992–93
2854	2855	7	F.90	WU	1991–92	2942	2943	8	F.92	WU	1992–93
2856	2857	7	F.90	WU	1991–92	2944	2945	8	F.92	WU	1992–93
2858	2859	7	F.90	WU	1991–92	2946	2947	8	F.92	WU	1992–93
2860	2861	7	F.90	WU	1991–92	2948	2949	8	F.92	WU	1992–93
2862	2863	7	F.90	WU	1991–92	2950	2951	8	F.92	WU	1992–93
2864	2865	7	F.90	WU	1991–92	2952	2953	8	F.92	WU	1992–93
2866	2867	7	F.90	WU	1991–92	2954	2955	8	F.92	WU	1992–93
2868	2869	7	F.90	WU	1991–92	2956	2957	8	F.92	WU	1992–93
2870	2871	7	F.90	WU	1991–92	2958	2959	8	F.92	WU	1992–93
2872	2873	7	F.90	WU	1991–92	2960	2961	8	F.92	WU	1992–93
2874	2875	7	F.90	WU	1991–92	2962	2963	8	F.92	WU	1992–93
2876	2877	7	F.90	WU	1991–92	2964	2965	8	F.92	WU	1992–93
2878	2879	7	F.90	WU	1991–92	2966	2967	8	F.92	WU	1992–93
2880	2881	7	F.90	WU	1991–92	2968	2969	8	F.92	WU	1992–93
2882	2883	8	F.90	WU	1991–92	2970	2971	8	F.92	WU	1992–93
2884	2885	8	F.90	WU	1991–92	2972	2973	8	F.92	WU	1992–93
2886	2887	8	F.90	WU	1991–92	2974	2975	8	F.92	WU	1992–93
2888	2889	8	F.90	WU	1991–92	2976	2977	8	F.92	WU	1992–93
2890	2891	8	F.90	WU	1991–92	2978	2979	8	F.92	WU	1992–93
2892	2893	8	F.90	WU	1991–92	2980	2981	8	F.92	WU	1992–93
2894	2895	8	F.90	WU	1991–92	2982	2983	8	F.92	WU	1992–93
2896	2897	8	F.90	WU	1991–92	2984	2985	8	F.92	WU	1992–93
2898	2899	8	F.90	WU	1991–92	2986	2987	8	F.92	WU	1992–93
2900	2901	8	F.90	WU	1991–92	2988	2989	8	F.92	WU	1992–93
2902	2903	8	F.90	WU	1991–92	2990	2991	8	F.92	WU	1992–93

Motor	Motor	Line	Type	Built By	Year	Motor	Motor	Line	Type	Built By	Year
2992	2993	8	F.92	WU	1992–93	3002	3003	8	F.92	WU	1992–93
2994	2995	8	F.92	WU	1992–93	3004	3005	8	F.92	WU	1992–93
2996	2997	8	F.92	WU	1992–93	3006	3007	8	F.92	WU	1992–93
2998	2999	8	F.92	WU	1992–93	3008	3009	8	F.92	WU	1992–93
3000	3001	8	F.92	WU	1992–93	3010	3011	8	F.92	WU	1992–93

A3L.82 & A3L.92 Stock Train Formations
Lines U1 and U2

Motor	Motor	Type	Built By	Year	Motor	Motor	Type	Built By	Year
538	539	A3L.92/3	ABB/WU	1995	598	599	A3L.92/2	ABB/WU	1994
540	541	A3L.92/3	ABB/WU	1995	600	601	A3L.92/2	ABB/WU	1994
542	543	A3L.92/3	ABB/WU	1995	602	603	A3L.92/2	ABB/WU	1994
544	545	A3L.92/3	ABB/WU	1995	604	605	A3L.92/1	ABB/WU	1992–93
546	547	A3L.92/3	ABB/WU	1995	606	607	A3L.92/1	ABB/WU	1992–93
548	549	A3L.92/3	ABB/WU	1995	608	609	A3L.92/1	ABB/WU	1992–93
550	551	A3L.92/3	ABB/WU	1995	610	611	A3L.92/1	ABB/WU	1992–93
552	553	A3L.92/3	ABB/WU	1995	612	613	A3L.92/1	ABB/WU	1992–93
554	555	A3L.92/2	ABB/WU	1994	614	615	A3L.92/1	ABB/WU	1992–93
556	557	A3L.92/2	ABB/WU	1994	616	617	A3L.92/1	ABB/WU	1992–93
558	559	A3L.92/2	ABB/WU	1994	618	619	A3L.92/1	ABB/WU	1992–93
560	561	A3L.92/2	ABB/WU	1994	620	621	A3L.92/1	ABB/WU	1992–93
562	563	A3L.92/2	ABB/WU	1994	622	623	A3L.92/1	ABB/WU	1992–93
564	565	A3L.92/2	ABB/WU	1994	624	625	A3L.92/1	ABB/WU	1992–93
566	567	A3L.92/2	ABB/WU	1994	626	627	A3L.92/1	ABB/WU	1992–93
568	569	A3L.92/2	ABB/WU	1994	628	629	A3L.92/1	ABB/WU	1992–93
570	571	A3L.92/2	ABB/WU	1994	630	631	A3L.92/1	ABB/WU	1992–93
572	573	A3L.92/2	ABB/WU	1994	632	633	A3L.92/1	ABB/WU	1992–93
574	575	A3L.92/2	ABB/WU	1994	634	635	A3L.92/1	ABB/WU	1992–93
576	577	A3L.92/2	ABB/WU	1994	636	637	A3L.92/1	ABB/WU	1992–93
578	579	A3L.92/2	ABB/WU	1994	638	639	A3L.92/1	ABB/WU	1992–93
580	581	A3L.92/2	ABB/WU	1994	640	641	A3L.82	O&K	1982–83
582	583	A3L.92/2	ABB/WU	1994	642	643	A3L.82	O&K	1982–83
584	585	A3L.92/2	ABB/WU	1994	644	645	A3L.82	O&K	1982–83
586	587	A3L.92/2	ABB/WU	1994	646	647	A3L.82	O&K	1982–83
588	589	A3L.92/2	ABB/WU	1994	648	649	A3L.82	O&K	1982–83
590	591	A3L.92/2	ABB/WU	1994	650	651	A3L.82	O&K	1982–83
592	593	A3L.92/2	ABB/WU	1994	652	653	A3L.82	O&K	1982–83
594	595	A3L.92/2	ABB/WU	1994	654	655	A3L.82	O&K	1982–83
596	597	A3L.92/2	ABB/WU	1994					

G Stock Train Formations
Lines U1 (occasionally), U2 & U15

Former Numbers	Motor	NDM	Former Numbers	Type	Built By	Year
135.998	266	267	135.999	G1/1	LEW	1989
135.996	268	269	135.997	G1/1	LEW	1989
135.994	270	271	135.995	G1/1	LEW	1989
135.992	272	273	135.993	G1/1	LEW	1989
135.990	274	275	135.991	G1/1	LEW	1989
135.988	276	277	135.989	G1/1	LEW	1989
135.986	278	279	135.987	G1/1	LEW	1989
135.984	280	281	135.985	G1/1	LEW	1989
135.982	282	283	135.983	G1/1	LEW	1989
135.980	284	285	135.981	G1/1	LEW	1989
135.978	286	287	135.979	G1/1	LEW	1989
135.976	288	289	135.977	G1/1	LEW	1989
135.974	290	291	135.975	G1/1	LEW	1989
135.972	292	293	135.973	G1/1	LEW	1989
135.970	294	295	135.971	G1/1	LEW	1989
135.968	296	297	135.969	G1/1	LEW	1989
135.966	298	299	135.967	G1/1	LEW	1989
135.964	300	301	135.965	G1/1	LEW	1989
135.962	302	303	135.963	G1/1	LEW	1989
135.960	304	305	135.961	G1/1	LEW	1989
135.958	306	307	135.959	G1/1	LEW	1989
135.956	308	309	135.957	G1/1	LEW	1989
135.954	310	311	135.955	G1/1	LEW	1989
135.952	312	313	135.953	G1/1	LEW	1989
135.950	314	315	135.951	G1/1	LEW	1989
135.948	316	317	135.949	G1/1	LEW	1989
135.946	318	319	135.947	G1/1	LEW	1989
135.944	320	321	135.945	G1/1	LEW	1989
135.942	322	323	135.943	G1/1	LEW	1989
135.940	324	325	135.941	G1/1	LEW	1989
135.938	326	327	135.939	G1/1	LEW	1988
135.936	328	329	135.937	G1/1	LEW	1988
135.934	330	331	135.935	G1/1	LEW	1988
135.932	332	333	135.933	G1/1	LEW	1988
135.930	334	335	135.931	G1/1	LEW	1988
135.928	336	337	135.929	G1/1	LEW	1988
135.926	338	339	135.927	G1/1	LEW	1988
135.924	340	341	135.925	G1/1	LEW	1988
135.922	342	343	135.923	G1/1	LEW	1988
135.920	344	345	135.921	G1/1	LEW	1988
135.918	346	347	135.919	G1/1	LEW	1988

Former Numbers	Motor	NDM	Former Numbers	Type	Built By	Year
135.916	348	349	135.917	G1/1	LEW	1988
135.914	350	351	135.915	G1/1	LEW	1988
135.912	352	353	135.913	G1/1	LEW	1988
135.910	354	355	135.911	G1/1	LEW	1988
135.908	356	357	135.909	G1/1	LEW	1988
135.906	358	359	135.907	G1/1	LEW	1988
135.904	360	361	135.905	G1/1	LEW	1988
135.902	362	363	135.903	G1/1	LEW	1988
135.900	364	365	135.901	G1/1	LEW	1988
135.898	366	367	135.899	G1/1	LEW	1989
135.896	368	369	135.897	G1/1	LEW	1989
135.884	372	373	135.885	GII	LEW	1983
135.878	378	379	135.879	GII	LEW	1983
135.876	380	381	135.877	GII	LEW	1983
135.870	386	387	135.871	GII	LEW	1983
135.866	388	389	135.867	GII	LEW	1983
135.860	392	393	135.861	G1	LEW	1983
135.856	396	397	135.857	G1	LEW	1982
135.854	398	399	135.855	G1	LEW	1982
135.852	400	401	135.853	G1	LEW	1981
135.850	402	403	135.851	G1	LEW	1981
135.844	408	409	135.845	G1	LEW	1981
135.842	410	411	135.843	G1	LEW	1981
135.840	412	413	135.841	G1	LEW	1981
135.824	426	427	135.825	G1	LEW	1980
135.822	428	429	135.823	G1	LEW	1980
135.820	430	431	135.821	G1	LEW	1980
135.818	432	433	135.819	G1	LEW	1980
135.816	434	435	135.817	G1	LEW	1980
135.814	436	437	135.815	G1	LEW	1980
135.810	440	441	135.811	G1	LEW	1980
135.808	442	443	135.809	G1	LEW	1980
135.806	444	445	135.807	G1	LEW	1980
135.804	446	447	135.805	G1	LEW	1980
135.802	448	449	135.803	G1	LEW	1980
135.800	450	451	135.801	G1	LEW	1980
135.796	454	455	135.797	G1	LEW	1980
135.794	456	457	135.795	G1	LEW	1979
135.778	470	471	135.779	G1	LEW	1979
135.772	476	477	135.773	G1	LEW	1978
135.764	484	485	135.765	G1	LEW	1978
135.760	488	489	135.761	G1	LEW	1978

Internal Working Trains – ex-passenger stock

No.	Ex.	Year	Type	Conv	Function	Location
4001	444	1949	A1 Narrow Profile	1968	Breakdown	Grunewald
4002	289	1925	A1 Narrow Profile	1978	Breakdown	Grunewald
4003	302	1926	A1 Narrow Profile	1978	Breakdown	Grunewald
4004	263	1926	B1 Large Profile	1981	Breakdown	Seestrasse
4005	127	1928	B2 Large Profile	1981	Breakdown	Seestrasse
4006	254	1926	B1 Large Profile	1975	Breakdown	Britz
4007	121	1927	B2 Large Profile	1975	Breakdown	Britz
4008	712.002	1929	A2 Narrow Profile	1976	Breakdown	Friedrichsfelde
4009	712.003	1929	A2 Narrow Profile	1989	Breakdown	Friedrichsfelde
4010	712.004	1929	A2 Narrow Profile	1976	Breakdown	Friedrichsfelde
4031	710.002	1926	A1 Narrow Profile	1980	Shunter	
4032	710.011	1926	A1 Narrow Profile	1980	Shunter	
4190	870	1949	A2 Narrow Profile	1974	Gauging	
4191	1368	1930	C2 Large Profile	1972	Gauging	

Bibliography

Berlin, the Biography of a City – A. Read and D. Fisher, Hutchinson, London, 1994.

The Fall of Berlin – A. Read and D. Fisher, Hutchinson, 1992.

Berliner U-Bahn – U. Lenke and U. Poppel, Alba Publikation GmbH, Düsseldorf.

125 Jahre Strassenbahnen in Berlin – S. Hilkenbach and W. Kramer, Alba 1990.

Berliner Omnibusse – D. Gammrath, Alba 1988.

S- und U-Bahn Architektur in Berlin – H-W Klünner, Senate of West Berlin, 1985.

60 Jahre U-Bahn Linie E – various authors, Arbeitsgemeinschaft Berliner U-Bahn, Berlin 1990.

Das Berliner U- und S-Bahnnetz, eine Geschichte in Streckenplänen – A. Gottwaldt, Argon, Berlin 1995.

Berlin Baut – No. 13 Published by the Senate of Berlin, Building Department, 1993 and 1995. (This publication deals with the reconnection of U2.)

50 Jahre BVG, 1929-1979 – BVG 1979.

Typisch Berlin, ein BVG Portrait – BVG 1987.

Tramway & Light Railway Atlas, Germany 1992 – LRTA London, 1993.

Periodicals

Berliner Verkehrsblätter – from 1984 to date.

Der Stadtverkehr – from 1979 to date.

VB Kompress (Modelleisenbahn-Verband der DDR) – Nos. 1, 2 & 3.

Abbreviations

General

ABOAG	Allgemeine Berliner Omnibus Aktien Gesellschaft
BEWAG	Berliner Elektrizitätswerke Aktien Gesellschaft
BLS	Betriebsleitstelle S-Bahn
BLU	Betriebsleitstelle U-Bahn
BMFT	Bundesministerium für Forschung und Technik
BVB	Kombinat Berliner Verkehrsbetriebe
BVG	Berliner Verkehrs-Betriebe
DB	Deutsche Bundesbahn
DBAG	Deutsche Bahn AG
DDR	Deutsche Demokratische Republik
DR	Deutsche Reichsbahn
DRG	Deutsche Reichsbahn Gesellschaft
EWAG	Elektrizitätswerke Aktien Gesellschaft
HVG	Havelbus Aktien Gesellschaft
Hochbahn	Gesellschaft für elektrische Hoch-und Untergrundbahnen
KPEV	Königliche Preussische Eisenbahn Verwaltung
S-Bahn	Schnellbahn
U-Bahn	Untergrundbahn
VdeR	Verwaltung des ehemaligen Reichsbahnvermogens
ViP	Verkehr in Potsdam

Manufacturers

ABB	ASEA-Brown Boveri
AEG	Allgemeine Elektrizitäts Gesellschaft Berlin-Hennigsdorf
ASF	AEG Schienenfahrzeuge Hennigsdorf (ex-AEG)
DWA	Deutsche Waggonbau AG
DWM	Deutsche Waggon-und Maschinenfabrik
LEW	Lokomotivbau Elektrotechnische Werke 'Hans Beimler', Hennigsdorf
MAN	Maschinenfabrik Augsburg-Nürnberg
MBB	Maschinenfarrik Messerschmidt-Bölkow-Blohm
O&K	Orenstein & Koppel
Siemens	Siemens Aktien Gesellschaft
UEG	Union-Elektrizitäts-Gesellschaft
WU	Waggon-Union GmbH